Wherefore comfort yourselves together, and edify one another, even as also ye do.

1 Thessalonians 5:11

Encouragers II
Walking with the Masters

by

Randall Franks

One of America's favorite TV cops shares

encouraging stories about his entertainment friends.

Peach Picked Publishing ISBN: 978-0-9849108-3-0
P.O. Box 42, Tunnel Hill, Georgia 30755
Editor: Rachel Brown Kirkland
Preliminary Column Editors: Stan Guess and Kevin Cummings
Photos unless otherwise noted © Randall Franks Media
Randall's front cover photo: © 1990 Randall Franks Media – Ned D. Burris
Randall's back cover photos: Police © 1990 Randall Franks Media – J. Alan Palmer
Fiddle © 1994 Randall Franks Media – Ned D. Burris
A portion of the proceeds from this book will be donated
to the Share America Foundation, Inc.
www.shareamericafoundation.org

Randall Franks performs for 10,000 fans at
Country Music Association Fan Fair in 1992.

Table of Contents

Encouragers

Table of Contents

Table of Contents

Preface

"Encouragers II : Walking with the Masters" is the second in a series of three books. They share experiences from throughout my life in entertainment and many of the friends I have come to know that God placed in my life. Beginning my musical career as a child, He allowed me to start on my adventures early. Many have asked me, "How have you done so much at your age?" Well, with the support of my late parents Floyd (1933–1987) and Pearl Franks (1926–2006), talents shared by God, and the doors that He opened for me to run through, I was blessed to do so many wonderful things. I've met so many of the greats in music, television, and just life in general who made an impact on me.

Within these pages I pay homage to so many who made it all possible, who inspired me, who gave me a helping hand or a bit of advice. By all means these are not all who played a role thus far in my life, and by leaving someone out I am not slighting their contribution. These are simply those with whom I had the best story or the most vivid memory to share.

Along with my stories are photos from my private collection, many never seen before in public, featuring some of the stars as we shared a moment in time. Some of those are from my work in the magic factory of MGM/UA that helped form the careers of so many of film's greatest talents. God opened the door for me on "In the Heat of the Night" to play a regular role in the popular Southern police series as "Officer Randy Goode."

To add to this project, I am including a collection of some of the favorite recipes of many of the celebrity friends included among other favorite recipes that are sure to please.

I pray these thoughts and stories encourage your life; they certainly were a great encouragement to me.

Who Are Encouragers?

A person that goes out of their way to let you know you can do what you set out to do.

Most of us have had parents and grandparents who probably fall in that category.

It is almost a given that someone charged with bringing up a child should have the sensibilities of an encourager.

I have been honored to find many encouragers in my life who have come along at different ages and with varying interests in seeing me succeed in different paths.

People I have admired. People who have been guides to me in the darkest of night, or the brightest of day.

First and foremost, one of the greatest encouragers I have ever come to know is Jesus. His light has lead millions now for 2,000 years. For this Georgia boy, he is always there to lean on, or to guide me through whatever comes my way.

My parents were encouragers to me. No matter what they faced — the Great Depression, war, meeting the needs of my brothers and I — they were always there doing what had to be done. They were the best parents they knew how to be. They gave us love, support, and guidance to the best of their abilities. While this does not sound unusual in the scheme of things, when you look at what is happening today with so many parents not fulfilling their parental responsibilities, my parents were truly stars. If yours are too, take a moment and let them know.

The earliest encouragers away from home we often find are as we take those first uncertain steps into the halls of learning and we sit down in a desk with our eyes, ears, and we hope minds open. Although the attention span is often short in our early years, I know the teachers do their very best to instill confidence in our own abilities.

At any given point in my schooling, I can find one teacher who stood out in giving me more than what was required. They would make whatever I wanted seem important. No matter how dumb the question was, they made it seem intelligent.

I still remember several elementary teachers — Ms. Crumbley,

Who Are Encouragers?

Ms. Johnson, Ms. Wallis, Ms. Brewer, Ms. Dennis, and the school librarian Ms. Mary Dantzler.

As I moved into high school, there were many who for a time made a difference: Nancy Grantham, Rozelle D'Orazio, Beverly Cole, Susan Via, and Gail Hunter.

One teacher in particular, because of his love of music, changed the direction of my life. Dr. Donald Grisier brought the violin into my life and set the stage for God to open so many doors.

Even as I entered college, there were professors who took the time to encourage me, though their classes were so large.

In the neighborhood where I grew up there were several who took an interest in what I was doing and encouraged me: Bessie Yarbray, Millie Dobbs, Baxter and Hazel Reed, Ed and Dot Mikell, Al and Jane Weidenmuller, Van McFall, Mary Burgess, and Nettie Fisher.

Eventually, I stepped out into the world beyond the safety of home and school and into the business and music worlds. There, I found so many more who gave me a hand.

My first employer, Joe Wyche, ran the local Dairy Queen near where I grew up outside Atlanta. He and the managers, David and Ed, gave me a chance to earn a little money. I was able to learn responsibility and how to deal with customers. There were so many other lessons. Thanks to their guidance, I soon became one of the youngest managers in the Dairy Queen system. I learned so much about business and life as I worked my way through school curling cones, flipping burgers, and counting money.

Musically, there were so many who nudged me along as I became a musician. First were other teachers: Jean Stiles, Caroline Worley, Eugene Akers, and Dallas Burrell.

Then there were the early performing mentors such as John and Debbie Farley, Doodle Thrower, Gene Daniell, Earle Wheeler, Keith Chambers, Elaine and Shorty Eager, T.P. and Sandra Hollomon, and so many more.

Once I grew in my efforts and caught the eye of Nashville, I was honored to have on-stage and off-stage legends take an interest in my talents. Among the initial cheerleaders were Bill Monroe, Josh

Who Are Encouragers?

Graves, Jim and Jesse McReynolds, Roy Acuff and Justin Tubb. The list extended as my career did. When I was still in my teens, Bill Monroe, the father of bluegrass music, took interest in this young fiddler. He spent many hours sharing his music with me. He arranged my first guest starring appearance for the Grand Ole Opry which began a long association with that musical institution. When an opening came available in his band, he asked me to join. Since I was in school, my time with the band was limited, but my friendship and my time as one of his students never ended until God gave him his final curtain call. He and his music are a light for millions around the world, but for me, he was my guide, my teacher, and my friend. He was truly a star to me.

Behind the scenes there was Jean Osborn, Joe Taylor, the Johnson Sisters, David McCormick, Jo Walker-Meador, Fran and Bill Boyd, Marge Meoli, Harold Bradley, Merle Kilgore, Linda Zuch, Gerald Roy, Jeff Goodwin, Martha Moore, Ronald and Joy Cotton, Carl Queen, Chris White, and Angie Acker. There were numerous music promoters — Strawberry Tipton, Vinson Dover, Vida and Gene Cox, Bob Pinyan and George Bales, Dillard Rogers, Gene and Betty Alford, Norman Adams and Tony Anderson, Wiley and Annette Rakestraw, Dan Daniel, Chuck and Diane Stearman, Charles Hamby, Dell Davis, Bertie Sullivan, and Lonnie and Peggy Knight, among others.

An ever-present partner in the life of a recording artist are engineers and studio owners. I was and am blessed with many friends who helped to create my sound and give me opportunities from Jim Crisp at Perfection Sound to Bill Turpin at Real to Reel, Rodney Brown at Treetop to Ben Hall at Home Place Studio, Ed E. Roland, Tag George, Brent Richardson, Bob and Babs Richardson, and Mike Clark among them.

When it comes to my move to television and film, it opened opportunities for so many others to take me under their wing. Initially music opened the doors and I landed numerous appearances on TV including joining the cast of "The Country Kids TV Series." Those credits allowed me to make my first steps into acting, thanks to so

Who Are Encouragers?

many. Among the earliest were Gail Houghton and Dee Voight, followed by "In the Heat of the Night" behind-the-scenes-guiders John Isabeau, Peter Salim, Eldon Burke, and James Griffin.

Then came those in front of the camera: Carroll O'Connor, Alan Autry, David Hart, and Geoffrey Thorne. O'Connor, TV's "Archie Bunker" and "Chief Gillespie," and Autry, "Bubba," both took an interest in me as a person and in my work. They took the time, along with many producers like David Moessinger, Jeri Taylor, and Walton Dornisch; directors like Salim, Larry Hagman, Harry Harris, Vince McEveety, and Leo Penn; and other actors to encourage me, teach me, and give me opportunities to go where a boy from Georgia could not even imagine — on "In the Heat of the Night."

They were followed by so many more industry professionals, including agents Kathy Hardegree, Edna Byers, Betty Clark, and Lynn-Moore Oliver.

As I entered my period in journalism, I found so many both who worked with me and those who read my work.

Now as I continue my journey, in acting I find encouragers among those who care about what I do. There are professionals such as Shay Bentley-Griffin, Melissa Goodman, Melinda Eisnaugle, Mystie Buice, friends from my hometown, music friends, and so many others.

To me, an encourager can be anyone who shares their God-given talents with others. They may be a good cook, a great mechanic, a successful salesperson, an inspiring clergyman, a visionary statesman or a cone-maker. They are all encouragers if they choose to be.

They all mean so much to me; each day is better because God sent them my way at some point when I needed their encouragement.

Why don't you take a look at the encouragers in your life? Let them know that your life is better because their light is shining on you. Is your light shining on those around you? If so, you can be an encourager too.

The Shape of Things to Come

Those who sculptured me

A Wander Through the Neighborhood

I could not have been more than four or five when I decided that Halloween could only be better the second time around. It was the day after Halloween. I was playing in the pine-paneled den in my Spiderman costume that I had worn so proudly the night before as my mother took me from house to house to gather an abundance of candy.

My mother, Pearl Franks, was busy ironing in the doorway of the den. She of course had the wooden ironing board with a daisy cover strategically placed to block my exit from the room. But like any four-year-old super hero, I anxiously watched for my opportunity to escape from my Spidy lair of captivity to face the legions of evil that needed vanquishing. When it came, I was out of there like a forty-pound cannonball and headed for the door.

Of course, at the time, I'm sure I gave no thought to doing anything wrong. In my four-year-old mind, I decided I wanted to have as much fun as I did the night before. So with my costume on and my bag emptied out, down the road I went.

I rang doorbells on my tiptoes, and knocked on doors. Everyone greeted me graciously. A few pointed out I was a little late. Most all managed to come up with something. Several folks even emptied what they had left in my bag. As I worked my way down the street, my mother realized that I was nowhere to be found and began what she later told me was a frantic search of the house and yard. She called the neighbors immediately around us, but most of them were at work so they had not come to the door when I rang.

Of course, I was oblivious to all this in my quest for a full bag, so I kept going. Our Wakefield Forest neighborhood in the northeast suburbs of Atlanta included one semicircle street with around fifty homes on one half with an intersecting street. With my little two legs, I had managed to work my way all the way down to the intersecting street and had started around the other half. My mother had already called my father at work, and I believe she might have called the police.

About that time, our next-door neighbor Fred Gross arrived home for lunch, and he had seen me rounding the corner. Immediately,

Encouragers

Randall Franks (fourth from right) and his kindergarten class ready to trick or treat

mother jumped in the car coming after me. It was not long before I was seated beside her in our light blue 1964 Chevy Malibu, my Spidy legs dangling off the front of the seat as I almost hid my little face down in the sack of candy — knowing that I had done something that I should not have done.

By the time I arrived home, I vaguely remember my dad, Floyd Franks, had arrived home from work. While much of what happened after is a blur in my childhood memory, I know that I did not enjoy that extra bag of candy as much as I thought I was going too — at least initially.

In the excitement of the costumes and candy, children often forget little things like the rules they need to remember like looking both ways before crossing the street, to trick or treat with an adult or responsible older child, and not to eat your candy until your parents or guardians have checked it out.

I am thankful that my parents cared enough about me to almost call out the National Guard when I disappeared on my little Halloween excursion. I was blessed to live in a community of caring people that looked after me as I wandered along. If I could go back and not put my mother and father through that, I would.

A Wander Through the Neighborhood

But you know, that was an awfully big bag of candy, and you should have seen those jawbreakers. They were good to keep me occupied while needing to stand up for the next few days ... Well, it is needless to say, I never did anything like that again.

It was just the neighborhood where a preschooler could wander freely without worry knowing folks were looking after him. I didn't have just one set of parents but easily an entire fire brigade full of them. There was hardly a household along our street that didn't have a hand in guiding my life forward — even if it was just encouraging me to go home. I did like to visit.

Other than those already mentioned, my extra neighborhood family were Al and Jane Weidenmuller, Dot and Ed Mikell, Joe and Van McFall, Baxter and Hazel Reed, Mr. Douglas, the Neils, the Wells, the Miners, the Loves, the Bounds and the Fishers and the Burgesses, who didn't live there but spent a lot of time with us.

They endured our neighborhood newspaper The Warwick Gazette, buying copies created with carbon paper by Bruce and Jenny Miner and I on the Miners' typewriter and everything thereafter I had to sell for school, scouts, or another purpose.

I spent endless hours at the Miners' playing, and they actually took me to one of my first folk music concerts featuring Joyce Brookshire.

My mother was close to Van McFall, Nettie Fisher, and Mary Burgess, which also resulted in me spending a lot of time at their

Nettie Fisher, Pearl Franks, Mary Burgess, and Van McFall in their DeKalb County Police uniforms

Encouragers

home and they at ours with their children along for the ride.

As I started my first business mowing yards at the age of nine, the Weidenmullers, the Mikells, and the Reeds all became regular customers. Mrs. Fisher helped me get customers in her neighborhood.

Through the years, I garnered a lot of sage advice and enjoyed tremendous quality time with many of them. The Mikells and the Weidenmullers were there supporting me consistently in all that I did well into adulthood.

Randall Franks (holding up gifts) celebrates a birthday with some neighborhood children and classmates.

Bessie

One of the greatest men of God of our time is undisputedly Billy Graham. The reach of his ministry has touched the four corners of the earth.

Bessie Yarbray

I once watched a message he delivered in Louisville, Kentucky. He shared his realization that he was finally old, when not too long ago he thought of himself as young. He went on to say that this point in life was "definitely not the golden years" — but that it is a good time to look back on life and come closer to God.

If we are blessed with long life, aging is something we all will face in either our own lives or that of our family members.

My first experiences with the effects of aging came from a childhood neighbor, Bessie Clack Yarbray.

Bessie was a regal lady who found strength in self-reliance. She was born at the turn of the last century in a farm-house less than five miles from our subdivision. She married and raised a family of (I think) five children.

When I met her as a toddler, she and her new husband Homer moved in across the street to begin their new life together near the age of seventy.

She stood around five feet, and if a strong wind blew through, it seemed she could catch hold and fly along.

She and Homer stood fast against the tide of concerns shared by both of their families over their late marriage.

While my memories of Homer are sketchy at best, I am told we had a fun relationship as he and Bessie treated me like a grandchild. My strongest memories fade in after Homer was called home. Bessie once again found herself starting over, this time in a place that she and Homer had hoped to share.

Bessie never learned to drive. She eventually sold Homer's car and relied on the kindness of friends and distant kin to get her to the store, doctor, and church. She would always find ways to repay their kindness so she would not be beholden to them.

She was a constant presence throughout my childhood. Really, throughout the childhood of all my friends in the neighborhood. Some days, the smell of fresh-baked oatmeal cookies would permeate the street in front of her house. This would always be an excuse to stop in to check on her and, of course, have a cookie or two or three.

She enjoyed watching her afternoon soaps and volunteering at Sardis United Methodist Church. She became a regular fixture among my mother's circle of friends as she helped with school events and attended graduations and scouting award banquets. Since we lived closer than any of her children, many of the first decisions concerning her care often would fall to my mother.

In the seventies, doctors told her she had colon cancer, which required surgery to remove or she would die. While in the hospital, she changed her mind, and when the nurses came by to give her a sedative before surgery she pretended to take it. She then left the hospital never to return. It was more than a decade before she would again see a doctor. She would live another twenty years, and to my knowledge, cancer was never again mentioned by any doctor.

Well into her eighties and nineties, Bessie cared for her yard by trimming hedges, raking, and mowing every week it was needed. "If I don't mow my yard, you know something is wrong," she would say.

She planted a garden each year that provided all her favorite, fresh vegetables.

With the bounty of her garden, she created dishes you would not believe. Thinking of her homemade soup makes my mouth water. The soup would not be complete without a slice of her piping-hot cornbread.

With the exception of an occasional change of a light bulb or flagging down the mailman or a neighbor to have them pull the cord on her push mower, Bessie didn't ask for much help.

Whenever sickness loomed, she always stressed to us: "No matter what, I do not want to leave my house."

Bessie

Bessie Yarbray in her kitchen

As we became busy with illnesses in our own family, other neighbors kindly stepped in to help Bessie whenever needed.

A broken hip which came while working in her yard in her mid nineties would finally begin a short period when she had to look to others for her day-to-day needs. She even regained her strength once again and stood on her own feet.

One of the last calls I received from her came at a time when she had missed taking her medicine properly and asked me if I saw the house going down the road. I stopped and looked to see if perhaps there was a house going down the road. There was not. We followed up to make sure that she was taking her medication properly.

About a year or so later, Bessie passed away.

She never left her home except for a few weeks following her broken hip. She was blessed with a strong self-reliance that made her keep pushing forward no matter what.

She reached the finish line her way, and with her faith in God still straight and strong.

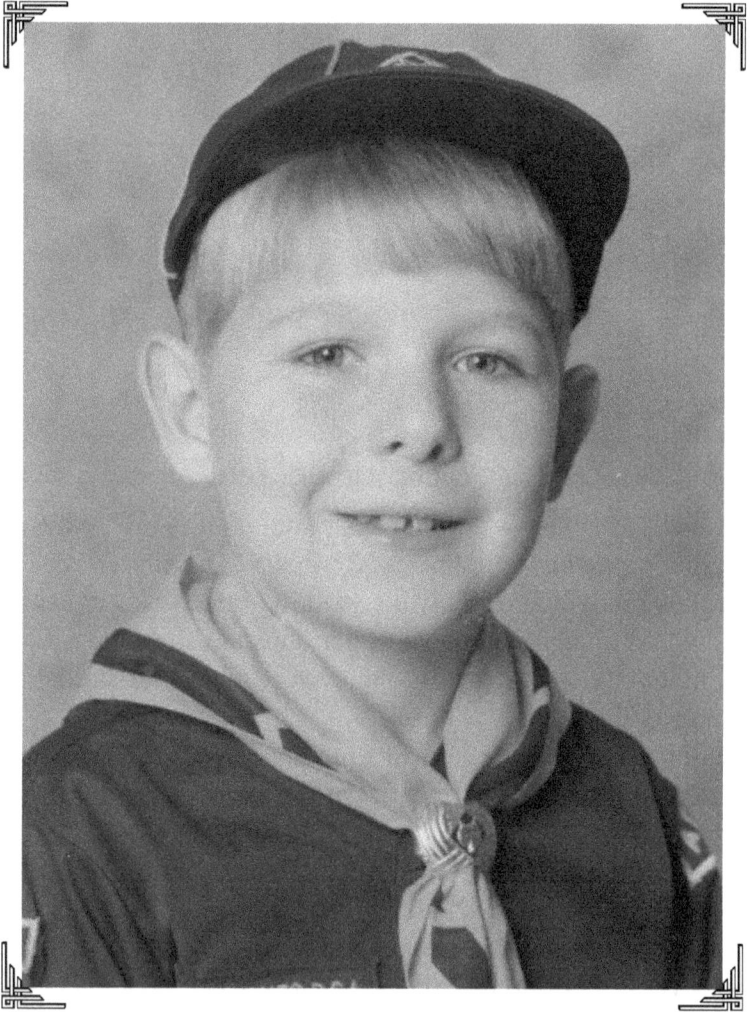

Randall Franks, fourth grade

A Grandma Not of My Blood

I opened the can and took a big breath through my nose. There was nothing quite like the smell of barbecue Charles Chips. I sure loved those chips as a boy; they were delivered like milk to the house and replenished into that metal can kept in the pantry. I took just one and placed it on my tongue and let the seasoning dissolve.

Then I took out a handful and placed them on my plate and on Millie's plate beside the sandwiches with thinly cut beef, brown mustard, tomato, and lettuce.

It was lunchtime and I was on a stay-over with my adopted grandmother Millie Dobbs.

Millie Dobbs
and Randall Franks

Millie was our next-door neighbor when I was a youth. When I was about six, our neighbors the Bounds moved to Florida and, to my initial disappointment, in moved a family with no children — Fred and Peggy Gross and Peggy's mother, Millie.

I am sure in many respects especially early on; I became a Southern Dennis the Menace to the Grosses as they settled in to their new home. Despite the lack of someone my age to play with, I soon found myself the focus of Millie, a retired nurse from New York City. On a side note, she told me about assisting Marilyn Monroe on a hospital stay. In just a short period of time, we had both found our way into each other's hearts.

Millie was what I would describe as puffy when I hugged her.

Since my folks had relocated to Atlanta for business, I was hours away from my grandparents, so it was wonderful having Millie in my life.

Often when Fred and Peggy went out of town, Millie would invite me to stay over. I would get to stay in the master bedroom suite. It was

Encouragers

always an adventure. I remember on one of my earliest visits, I opened the wrong door by mistake and began a head over foot tumble into the basement. I didn't get hurt though. I landed on my head. So if you wonder why I am still a bit off, that would be the reason. Actually, I limped away from the fall with a stumped toe.

Later I would learn the basement was Fred's domain where he kept his model train and 78-rpm record collections. I seldom got the chance to see those things, although it was a treat when I was allowed.

Millie was an amateur artist who loved painting and making crafts with her hands, and she often brought me into what she was doing to teach me and give me a try at it. She loved to play cards and she taught me as well — solitaire and gin rummy. We would often pass hours playing, especially when my Uncle Waymond Sherrill came to visit. Millie would always join our family for evenings of card- and game-playing.

Another one of her passions is still part of my life — mysteries — Agatha Christie among others.

Every few months, Millie would treat us both to a meal out and we would walk a little more than a mile to Brannigan's Irish Restaurant and have lunch. I would get this huge hamburger covered with mushrooms and everything imaginable.

As I grew and our family celebrated the milestones, Millie was there — birthdays, elementary graduation, Eagle Scout ceremony, and awards — until one day, Fred, Peggy, and Millie moved to Florida. I was in my teens by then and our connection remained via letters, cards, and holiday greetings.

One day, mother received a call from Peggy to let us know that Millie had died. My initial impulse was to go and be there with them. That is after all what we did in our family. We gathered, sat up with the dead, ate a lot, remembered, and cried as they were buried.

Peggy thanked me for the thought but said there was no need for us to make the trip down. As best I recall, Millie was cremated.

My adopted grandmother Millie was gone. My mom encouraged me to put away the things that she had shared with me, some paintings, needlepoint, an afghan, her letters, a handmade bell she had gotten

A Grandma Not of My Blood

from her friend Willie. So I did. You know, I am still saving them, like I simply put Millie's things away where I could keep my memory of her just the way it was.

I know that my childhood would not have been as full without the New York perspective that Millie brought to me — an appreciation of seeing more than what was just at my fingertips.

Millie gave me something no one else

Randall Franks and Millie Dobbs at Randall's Eagle Scout Ceremony

had before outside my family — she taught me that unconditional love didn't have to be born in blood. She became part of my family and shared time, encouragement, some of my greatest childhood moments, and an amazing love for life.

For we have great joy and consolation in thy love, because the bowels of the saints are refreshed by thee, brother.

Philemon 1:7

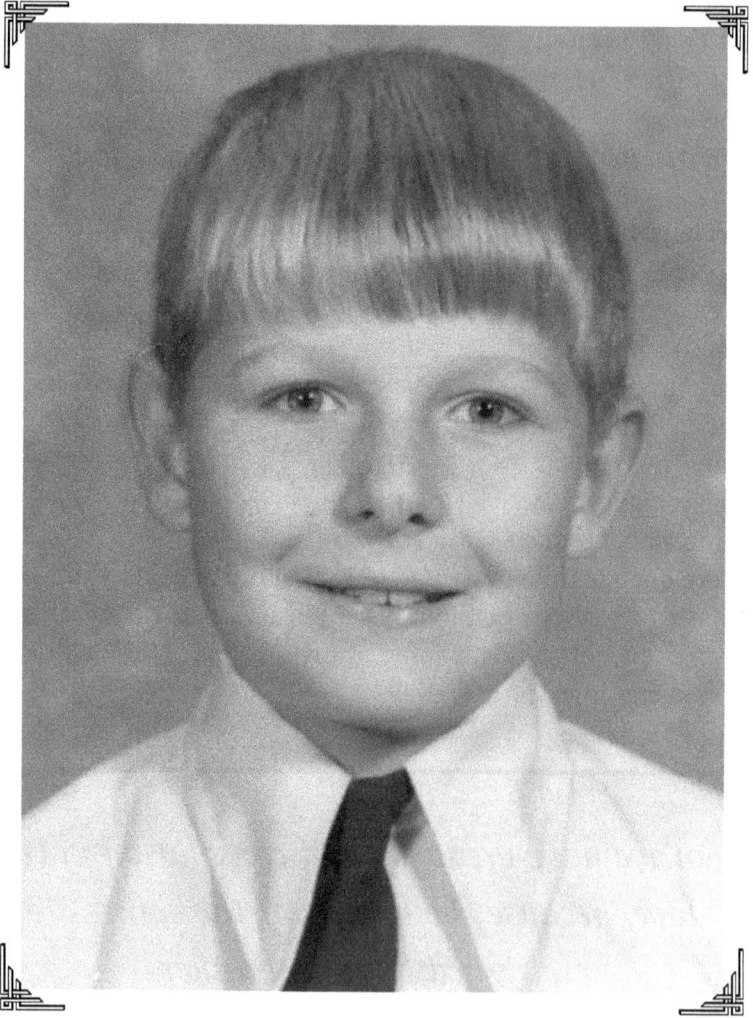

Randall Franks, fifth grade

A Shave and a Haircut

As I sat and squirmed in my chair trying to scratch a place in the middle of my back, I wasn't very happy that I made a trip to get a haircut. Have you ever noticed when you go to the barber that those little hairs that fall inside your shirt collar can make you itch for the rest of the day?

It kind of makes you understand the "hippie" movement, at least the hair part of it. I never understood my middle brother Alan's desire to have a six-inch afro. It must have been somewhere in the early seventies when I ran in from playing down the street to find my brother sitting in the living room looking like he had a fight with an electric toaster and lost.

Now, when I was growing up, men didn't go to a salon. A salon was for women. That's where womenfolk went to get their hair glued in place before they went to church on Sunday.

Back then, menfolk went to barber shops. If a man was caught going in to a beauty salon, it took a month of Sundays to live it down.

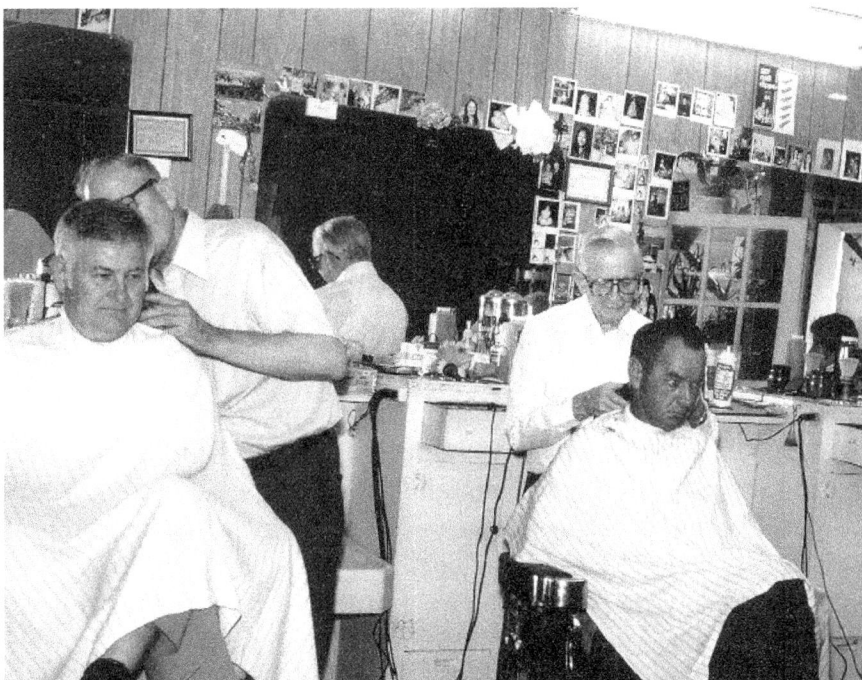

© 1979 Randall Franks

Mr. Saxon (right) gives a haircut in Chamblee, Georgia.

Encouragers

I often wonder why folks go to a salon to get their hair styled. They can do most anything there from your hair to your nails. They even got them places where you can get a full body wrap.

While memories of my first haircut have faded, I am told that I was really not too much of a squirmer in the barber's chair. I knew that if I didn't behave that would be my last time sitting down for a while.

After our family moved from the big city of Little Five Points out to the country in Chamblee, my dad and I settled on going to a barber named Mr. Andrew Saxon. Mr. Saxon cut my hair from my third birthday all the way through my senior year in high school.

One thing I have learned in my life is that loyalty to a barber is one of the most important choices a man can make. No matter where Mr. Saxon moved his practice through the years, that is where we went to get our hair cut.

Haircuts back then didn't cost an arm and a leg either. It took me years not to cringe when pulling more than two dollars out of my pocket for a haircut.

Randall

I understand the old barbershop in a basement on Main Street had been in business since the days of Civil War reconstruction. As I sat in a red leather swivel barber chair, I would look up above the mirrors on the wall and imagine the shotguns which I was told once were mounted above each barber chair in case some restless mountaineer needed to be reminded that he was in town. Hill folk would ride into town and not only get a haircut, shave, and a boot shine, but take a shower and house their horse out back while they were in town.

Mr. Saxon always managed to keep my dad and I properly trimmed. After my cut, I would always help out by sweeping up the hair clippings on the gray tile floor. Through the years, it was amazing how I always seemed to sweep up a dime or two to put in the old red carousel Coca-Cola machine when I was done.

Through the years, Mr. Saxon imparted many words of wisdom on this impressionable lad. Probably the lesson that stuck the most was, "Always remember, no matter who you meet in life, your mom and dad

A Shave and a Haircut

will be the best friends you will ever have."

By the time I had reached my senior year, Mr. Saxon was growing near retirement. While he was once a whiz, time was taking its toll. The loyalty within me insisted that he would be the one to cut my hair before my senior photos were taken. Unfortunately, that haircut left a lasting memory and was not a great testament to his many years of talented barbering. By the time I reached Georgia State University, trends in the outside world were making franchise style shops the place where people went for a trim. It was difficult for me to take my first steps into such a place, but eventually I did. Unlike the old barbershop, almost every time you went in, there would be a different butcher on duty.

As my musical star began to rise, a fellow musician from Chicago, Sue Koskela, had taken up the trade and become an award-winning stylist. Fortunately for me, she was kind enough to take me on as a client and would always travel in to handle photo shoots and album covers. She settled near Knoxville for many years, and I would regu-

© 1990 Randall Franks Media

Sue Koskela gives Randall a final look during the filming of "Handshakes and Smiles" in 1990.

larly make the six-hour round trip from Atlanta to have her work her magic. I am not exaggerating; what she did was magic. I knew when I walked out of there, I would not have to do anything to my hair and I would be sporting whatever latest style suited my look and shape of my face. Every time I went elsewhere, I usually looked like a cross between the Frankenstein monster and "Mo" from the Three Stooges.

When I joined the cast of "In the Heat of the Night" as "Officer Randy Goode," my head and hair became the responsibility of whichever hair and makeup artists were chosen to oversee my look. They had to make sure that we actors looked consistent throughout scenes that were filmed out of sequence. In one of those happenstance moments, we got a new and

Randall Franks (center) works on filming "Heart of Gold" on "In the Heat of the Night" with Geoffrey Thorne (left) and Alan Autry.

© 1990 Randall Franks Media

short-lived hair artist who decided to give me a different look for an episode entitled "Heart of Gold." I had one of my largest feature appearances of the early series. It was amazing to me how detrimental that look on camera was for me. I never realized until that point how much a person's hairstyle has to do with how they are perceived by other people.

Good grooming is something we can all do to make the world a better place, but finding a good barber these days can be as hard as finding a six-ounce bottle of Coca-Cola for a dime.

Can the Wisdom of a Lifetime Be Shared?

I was out buying tomato plants for the garden and it brought back memories of my thirteenth summer. I was in Boy Scouts and took on a project to teach crafts at Ashton Woods Convalescent Center a few miles from my home under the supervision of activities director Maureen Gruber. I remember being excited to get to teach leatherwork and other crafts to the residents. While a few took part, I remember after a while my interest turned from teaching to learning.

Mr. Farnell

Many of my free hours at the center were spent helping Mr. Farnell with the community vegetable garden. He was confined to his wheelchair, but with his knowledge and my arms, we raised an outstanding garden that year. I don't think I've ever been that successful with tomatoes, peppers, squash, and the like. That summer, he shared with me many stories of his life, his work with A&P grocery. Largely, he taught me how to appreciate the beauty of life — the joy of helping God make something grow.

Many of the gardening techniques he shared with me are still with me today.

Many of the residents made a lasting impression on me that year.

Mrs. McMahan was a simple joy to be around. She was the type of person who could just make you smile when she walked in the room. In spite of her battles with bad health, her outlook was always uplifting. From her, I learned that even the worst day can be faced with a smile.

Mr. and Mrs. Boxley both lived in the center. To me, they seemed

Mrs. McMahan

33

Encouragers

Mrs. Boxley

like a wonderful couple. They both had a spirit to enjoy life. They took each moment and did all they could with it. They both shared a passion for bird watching. They shared it with me. I still have a bird book Mrs. Boxley gave to me after Mr. Boxley passed away. I once saw a most unique bird with blue back and crimson front. There's not a day that I see a bird I've never seen before that those two don't cross my mind.

Mrs. Petit was one of the first severe stroke patients with whom I spent time. She had lost the use of one side of her body and spoke only with great effort. I learned the importance of perseverance from her. No matter what craft project we undertook, she made every effort to do her part.

There were dozens of patients that summer who I met and who became a part of my childhood. Many shared with me bits and pieces of their knowledge, their wisdom. Many were glad to share the company of a young person who was sincerely interested in them.

Mrs. Petit

A Boy Scout project brought me there, but it was the people who kept me coming back for years to come. Eventually, the folks I had grown close to were all called home. I often wish we could visit today, talk about where I've been and how they played a part in making me who I am today. I guess they are with me, even though I can not speak with them. They speak to me in memories, in the things they taught me. When I'm digging in the garden to plant the tomatoes, I can still envision Mr. Farnell sitting next to me saying "Dig a little deeper son, those roots need room to grow."

I often wonder what wisdom I will leave on this earth once I'm gone. Who will remember the things that were important to me? Will I leave a legacy of wisdom? I hope so, because within me, there are so

Can the Wisdom of a Lifetime Be Shared?

many people who I would like to see live on in what I share.

If you have never taken the time to visit with older members of your family, church, or community, I encourage you to spend some time with them. Listen to their stories, even though you think you may have heard them a thousand times. When they are gone, you will struggle to bring those moments back in your mind. You may even wish you had written down the wisdom they shared.

Oftentimes with the people that we see the most, we neglect to cherish the times and wisdom they are sharing.

Wisdom can be shared. It can be passed from one to another, if only we are open to learning. Sometimes, only with age the wisdom of what has been shared with us will become apparent. But it is never too early to start accumulating shared wisdom. Someday, it will come in handy.

Let no corrupt communication proceed out of your mouth, but that which is good to the use of edifying, that it may minister grace unto the hearer.

Ephesians 4:29

The Peachtree Pickers — 1980
From left are Cathy Phillips, Mark Nelson
and Randall Franks.

Summer Jobs — Life Lessons

As the school year comes to a close, my mind always wanders to days at Dairy Queen No. 8 on Clairmont Road near Chamblee. I spent my entire teenage life and college years working at that establishment. For a youth growing up in my community, the Dairy Queen was the place to be. It was owned by Joe Wyche.

Joe was a boss who gave a lot of youth a chance they might not have gotten elsewhere. I know there were many times he kept teenagers on the payroll not because he needed them but because he thought they needed something stable in their lives.

Joe, a Georgia Tech graduate, had spent several years with the Dairy Queen corporation building Dairy Queens all over the world. He even was there in the late fifties as the company laid the blocks for a neighborhood walk-up ice cream store which would later feature the Brazier burgers with all the fixings, tenderloin sandwiches, and onion rings. He decided to purchase the franchise area.

Joe, an avid sports fan, happily watched his sons, Sam

Joe and Barbara Wyche

and Bubba, go on to play college and professional football. Sam would eventually be the head coach of the Cincinnati Bengals and then a network sports commentator.

Joe and his late wife Barbara ran the store. Of course, they had several able-bodied managers and adult employees.

Manager David Payne originally hired me. It was the first summer I was old enough to qualify for working. I'll never forget how nervous I was at the interview. But David hired me, and I was flung to the

Encouragers

Ellen Hawley

Payne

wolves. What I mean is, I jumped in feet-first with the able assistance of another experienced Dairy Queen worker, who happened to be long-time friend and just slightly older than me Rhonda Fisher.

One of my first duties was cleaning out the storage refrigerator in the topping cooler. Much like Andy Griffith in "No Time for Sergeants," having the honor of such a duty elated me. It would be much later that I would find that cleaning that refrigerator was a close second to Griffith's latrine duty. Slowly, I was taught how to make each of the Dairy Queen favorites, "The Peanut Buster Parfait," "The Banana Split," "The Strawberry Shortcake," three sizes of cones and every imaginable flavor of milkshake from pineapple to peanut butter.

It was not long before I mastered the Dairy Queen cone curl. Although it has been years, I think it is like riding a bicycle. I believe I could still draw a cone pretty close to its exact weight and proportions. Yes, everything we made was to meet certain specifications.

I began my job at $1.65 an hour, which I am sure seems like not much by today's standards, but it was for me and I was glad to get it.

After David left, he was replaced by biker Ed Cross.

Ed arrived his first day on his Harley Davidson, dressed in black. He had long hair and tattoos.

While the biker images had influenced a state of caution in my youthful thinking, through the years, I got to know Ed. He changed that image as I found him to be someone you could depend on with your life. One thing about it, the teenagers who passed through would not even attempt to pull any shenanigans on Ed or Joe. I learned a lot about how to be a leader and a boss from both of them.

Ellen Hawley

Ed Cross

After several years on the job, at various times, I moved into the position of assistant day manager and night manager. I was told I was one of the youngest in the system. I even worked the early shift with morning manager Ellen Hawley as she rolled out the biscuits for breakfast and Becky Pirkle who cooked the bacon and ham on the grill. What I learned about hiring, firing, working with, and managing thirty-two employees of all ages is still part of me.

As my music career grew, Ed, Joe, and Virginia Sapp, who also was a manager, all accommodated my touring schedule, allowing me to be on the road. I seldom worked a Friday or Saturday night, which was unusual in the fast food business since those were the busiest times. But I was usually on stage somewhere pulling my fiddle bow across the strings.

When Joe decided to retire, he sold the store. It was a sad day for all of us. I stayed on for a while as did several of the employees. When I finally left Dairy Queen, it was like leaving a family.

I still find myself waxing nostalgic about early morning suppers with Joe, Barbara, and Virginia at Denny's after closing; midnight movies with all the crew; handing a well-curled cone to a little kid to see it gobbled up in one bite; and the exhaustion following a ninety-nine-cent special on banana splits.

I would not trade one hour I spent at the Dairy Queen for the finest job on Wall Street or one cent more than I earned.

So teens, don't be afraid to take those summer jobs you think are low paying. You might just learn something that will change your life.

Ointment and perfume rejoice the heart: so doth the sweetness of a man's friend by hearty counsel.

Proverbs 27:9

Randall Franks

All Day Singing and Dinner on the Grounds

Pickin' and Grinnin' Friends

Country, Bluegrass, Gospel, Rock 'n' Roll

Pickin' and Grinnin' Friends
Country Music

The Peachtree Pickers — 1982
From left are Jeff Blalock, Mark Nelson,
Wes Freeman and Randall Franks.

© 1982 Randall Franks Media – Wayne W. Daniel

The Country Music Association

Jo Walker-Meador

Someone who pushed forward the country music industry throughout my youth was Jo Walker-Meador. When the Country Music Association began in 1958, she became its secretary and by 1961 was its executive director. Her work serving the board of the organization helped bring into existence the Country Music Hall of Fame and the annual televised Country Music Association Awards.

In Jo, I saw someone who loved those who cared for country music, whether it was the artists, the fans, or the industry executives. It was the music that it was all about.

Cotton Carrier sponsored me to become a member of the Country Music Association in the 1970s, and I soon found myself learning more about all those who helped make things happen. The Country Music Association coordinated Country Music Fan Fair in a partnership with the Grand Ole Opry by the time I started participating.

So each year, as other country music artists did, we gave a full week to the fans with the help of those two organizations. We signed autographs in fan club booths and record company booths and did shows and interviews. Between twenty-thousand and thirty-thousand people would come from all around the world to the fairgrounds to experience what I would describe as a county fair where the exhibits were country music performers. Eventually as the event grew and moved back to downtown Nashville in 2002 the attendance exceeded 125,000.

When I landed my role on "In the Heat of the Night," one of the first people I went to see was Jo Walker-Meador. I knew Jo cared about seeing all those who performed country music excel at what they were doing. I hoped at that time my association with the show and with NBC might offer ways to raise the visibility of country music and of course hoped my association with country music might also open more doors for me.

Jo made sure everyone at the CMA knew who I was and what I was doing. Thanks to all the CMA staff who worked with Jo — Ed

Encouragers

Benson, Tammy Genovese, Janet Bozeman, Helen Farmer, Teresa George, and Janet Williams — they included my successes in the CMA CloseUp Magazine for all the membership to see almost monthly and kept me informed about events in which I should participate.

Jo retired from the CMA in 1991, but she graciously made sure that I had a meeting with her successor, Ed Benson, who then continued encouraging my efforts throughout his tenure.

Through the years, I found so many CMA staffers that encouraged my efforts and helped me such as those who worked in special events and public relations — Angie Acker, Bobette Dudley, Mandy Wilson, and so many others.

Through the years even after her retirement, Jo has continued to stay in contact by cheering my successes with notes.

I am sure I was not unique among my brothers and sisters in country music. I am sure that Jo extended the interest and care that she shared with me to many in our industry.

I was privileged that my career in Nashville and ultimately in Hollywood came under part of Jo's watch.

But Jesus turned him about, and when he saw her, he said, **Daughter, be of good comfort; thy faith hath made thee whole.** *And the woman was made whole from that hour.*

Matthew 9:22

My Opry Home

You might ask how a company can be an encourager. Well, when it's the Grand Ole Opry ®, it is. It began with the music and entertainment the show provided in my youth over 650 WSM as I tried to pull it in over the airwaves with my transistor radio.

As I grew as a musician and singer, it was the goal; to perform for the Opry meant that you had achieved a standard in your artistry that you were welcome on the national stage.

The Opry has seen its transformation, as has much of society. The passage of time has changed the faces of the legends and the management that guided its route and guarded its entry doors.

As I was growing up, there was not much room in country music for youth performers.

The last major success was my friend Tanya Tucker in the early 1970s. It is understandable since in many respects in that era there were two types of venues that the artists played — auditoriums and honky tonks. So if you had a youth, you cut out many of the potential venues.

My growth in the industry found its way into bluegrass and gospel which had more opportunities for youth, but it still made it much more difficult to gain Nashville's attention because

Former Grand Ole Opry manager Hal Durham and Randall Franks

they were steering away from those segments of the genre to focus where greater opportunities seemed to be present, leaving the established artists in those fields to fend for themselves. As a result, genres were creating their own industries — venues, record companies, media companies, etc.

So I did what I knew to do — play the music where I could, and keep plowing towards the goal — the Grand Ole Opry.

47

Encouragers

My entrance came through two routes, one that took me to Bill Monroe and the other to Roy Acuff. In both cases, I found men who graciously stood in my corner and cheered me onto the stages of the Grand Ole Opry, allowing me the opportunity to grow among the Opry family for many years.

Eventually, those reins were passed to Opry manager Hal Durham, who held them all along anyway, and he made places for me. His eventual successors, Jerry Strobel and Steve Buchanan, even had a hand in it for a while.

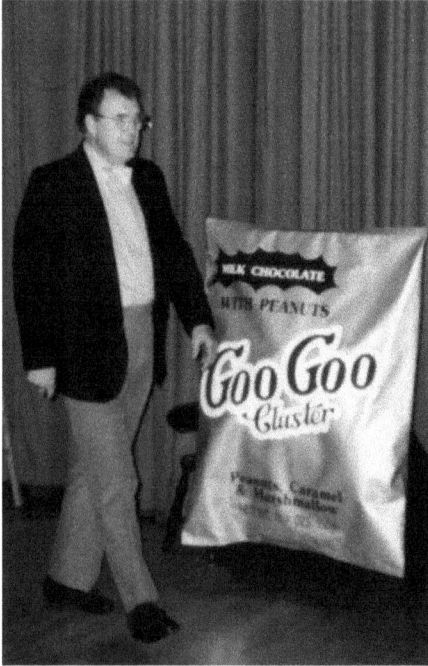

Grand Ole Opry announcer Hairl Hensley with one of my favorite sponsors

Even when I wasn't performing, if I was in town on a Friday or Saturday, I was backstage visiting, learning, and connecting with other artists and industry leaders.

I certainly believed the key to remaining part of the family over time was being present, and I did whenever possible.

Of course, entrance into the backstage of the venue was coordinated by security both at the parking lot gate and the door. For many years, Bobby Rose and Mr. Van Dame were there to greet you or send you on your way if you were not on the list.

Backstage, it was always electric. Music friends gathered every few feet sharing the latest news, lemonade flowing in the main backstage waiting room, artists warming up in all the dressing rooms with folks hanging around the doors listening.

Then you could step into the darkness of backstage and make your way up to the ropes to watch whomever was sharing their portion on

My Opry Home

stage.

I spent a lot of time in that darkness peering out at center stage and those sitting in the audience looking back.

I developed a dual identity in essence over my association — as a bluegrass entertainer but also as a fiddler/comedian — that allowed me to fit alongside the other Opry stars either using my own band or a staff band.

From about 1984 until the late 1990s, I proudly shared the stage with almost every

Randall Franks and Keith Bilbrey in 2011, announcer for RFD-TV's "Larry's Country Diner," formerly of the Grand Ole Opry and WSM.

Opry star of the era whether in Nashville or elsewhere. There was not one of them that I did not learn something from by watching and listening.

Randall Franks and Kyle Cantrell in 1997, former Grand Ole Opry and WSM announcer. He is currently heard on Sirius Satellite Radio.

The Opry provided a unique family in which to grow, learn, fail, and succeed; and I was honored to have been there.

The announcers made a point to always make me feel at home and build me up on stage and on their radio shows, and I am so grateful to them all. Those I worked closely with were Grant Turner, Hairl Hensley, Keith Bilbrey, and Kyle Cantrell.

The Carol Lee Singers

Encouragers

backed the artists as they performed on the stage of the Opry. Their leader, Carol Lee Cooper, was a good friend and supporter adding her group's sound to several of my recordings through the years as well as some I produced for others. Carol Lee also encouraged me to journal and keep notes about my entertainment experiences.

Carol Lee Cooper studies the work of her fellow Carol Lee Singers — Dennis McCall and Herman Harper — as they record a session with Randall Franks at Ben Hall's Home Place Studio in 1995.

One of my favorite memories after years of association with the Opry family is when I was making an appearance and Roxanne Russell, who hosted Opry Notes for TNN, came out to cover me at the event. I thought I had finally arrived and was fully accepted as part of the family.

I knew I would never be inducted, because my musical career would never produce the top country song that for so long was the initial benchmark for consideration, but I had hopes that if I continued in my efforts, one day I might come in another door. Slowly through the 1990s as we said goodbye to those artists who held on so tightly to the show through their influence, I could see the changes. The bustling backstage became less that way as the stars became more modern in their approach to show business.

The management reformatted the show to appeal to a younger audience, and thus it continues building and adding a new base of Opry fans. While 2002 was when I last appeared for an Opry-related event, I still consider myself part of the Opry family. Who knows? Maybe one day, good Lord willin' and the creeks don't rise, as Arnold said, "I'll be back."

The King of Country Music — Roy Acuff

While today others may look to the latest big-selling artist on the country stations as the king, for me there will only be one. Mr. Roy Acuff (1903–1992) reigned as a country star for fifty-four years from 1938 to 1992.

Of course, after a time, he was afforded the well-earned title of the King of Country Music, and from

Randall Franks and Roy Acuff share a moment backstage at the Grand Ole Opry in 1991.

Dressing Room #1 he guided the Grand Ole Opry ® family each week through the personal and professional ups and downs all the artists faced. He helped to keep the focus on one thing — the people who attended and tuned in to the Grand Ole Opry each week.

My first introduction to Roy Acuff came both through radio and television watching Hee Haw ® and the big country award shows and listening to the Opry radio show.

As a boy, I learned to play his first big song, "The Great Speckled Bird," on the fiddle. Then came "The Wabash Cannonball," which I probably sang a thousand times on my early performances.

Roy loved fiddling and fiddle players, so as I grew stronger in fiddle contests, eventually we tried our hand in the Grand Master Fiddler Championship. In those days, the competitors were much older, so younger fiddlers were encouraged no matter their skill level. Roy was a tremendous supporter of the events sponsored by the Grand Ole Opry.

My late father, Floyd, initially gained Roy's interest in my music. I still remember one night backstage at the Opry watching from one side of the stage how as Roy saw my father, he left the other side of

51

the stage and made a beeline to my father and they had a long visit as I watched in amazement. My father didn't even tell me that they knew one another.

When I was invited to make my first guest appearance for the Grand Ole Opry in 1984, needless to say I was nervous. As my group stood on the stage entertaining the crowd, I looked over in the wings and there was Roy smiling back at me. His enthusiasm cheered me on as I made my debut.

Through the next eight years of his life, as I returned to the Opry to visit backstage or to make a guest appearance for one of their programs, Roy welcomed me into his dressing room. He would ask me how my life was going, what was new in my career. As my musical career opened doors into acting, he even took the time to sit down in his dressing room with me and share some of his early Hollywood experiences with Republic Pictures. I was extremely excited when I was able to bring by some of my "In the Heat of the Night" co-stars to meet him in 1991.

Through those years I also came to know the members of his band — the Smoky Mountain Boys — and was privileged to call many of them friend.

After his passing, the music community gathered at the now gone Roy Acuff Theater at Opryland to say goodbye. I remember it like it was yesterday. As my association with the Opry continued, I greatly felt his absence. Country music could sure use someone today like him.

© 1991 Randall Franks Media – Donna Tracy

Alan Autry, Randall Franks, Roy Acuff, and David Hart on November 21, 1991

ET Record Shop's Midnight Jamboree

In my earliest memories of turning on the Grand Ole Opry on Saturday nights, the show would always be followed by yet another iconic show of American radio — the Ernest Tubb Midnight Jamboree.

One of my fondest boyhood memories comes from one of our family's trips to Music City. The Grand Ole Opry was our first stop.

The entire event just consumed me — the curtains, the stage, and the stars. Then one of the greatest performers, Ernest Tubb (1914–1984) hit the stage, captivating this young boy.

In his career, Tubb (and his Texas Troubadours) sang of a "Waltz Across Texas" and delighted the world with his self-penned "Walkin' the Floor Over You" and songs such as "Slippin' Around," "Rainbow at Midnight," and "Blue Eyed Elaine." The Grand Ole Opry star opened the Ernest Tubb Record Shop in Nashville and began the Midnight Jamboree on WSM following the Opry in the late forties.

Courtesy Katona Productions, Inc.

Grand Ole Opry star
Ernest Tubb

Tubb's film appearances included Charles Starrett's Fighting Buckeroos and Ridin' West.

As he stood on the stage with a few words and a wave of his hand,

Encouragers

he introduced another favorite of mine, Loretta Lynn. That's something I will always remember. To me, she has always been one of the greatest class acts in country music.

The Opry was just the first stop. Then we were off to the Ernest Tubb Record Shop for the Midnight Jamboree in the midst of an abundance of records. I never dreamed that I would be a part of this special time-honored tradition.

Randall Franks delivers some food at the ET Fan Appreciation Day in 1991.

That was where it really hit me — the sights and sounds of the musicians tuning and waiting for the broadcast to start. The stars were within an arm's length, where you could reach out and touch them. This was better than the Opry.

In many ways, instead of me touching them, they reached out and lifted me into their world of making a difference in the lives of millions through a desire to share the music God shared with me. The show continues to air on WSM 650 AM at midnight (CST).

As I traveled after appearing with Grand Ole Opry star Jesse McReynolds in 2008, I tuned in and listened to Leona Williams co-

ET Record Shop's Midnight Jamboree

host a show just as entertaining, just as magical as it ever was.

The Midnight Jamboree's physical home, the Texas Troubadour Theater adjacent to its Music Valley Village store, is much plusher than the in-store stages from many years ago, yet the music is still the focus.

Randall Franks performs on the Midnight Jamboree in 1991.

© 1991 Randall Franks Media

When I returned to films and music full-time in 2009, the Midnight Jamboree was the first Nashville venue to welcome me back where I co-starred with Kathy Mattea.

I felt as honored and as blessed as the first time I walked on the stage.

I was honored many times to participate in the Ernest Tubb Record Shop Fan Appreciation Day, where the stars serve and perform, and I appeared on the

Randall Franks visits with Justin Tubb at Fan Fair in 1991.

© 1991 Randall Franks Media – Donna Tracy

Encouragers

Midnight Jamboree with Grand Ole Opry star Justin Tubb (1935-1998), Ernest's son.

Justin joined the Opry in 1955 and entertained throughout his life. Early in his career, he enjoyed success with some duets with Goldie Hill including one of my favorites, "Looking Back to See." One of his solo hits was "I Gotta Go Get My Baby." Among his major songwriting successes was "Lonesome 7-7203."

He was always someone who took a little time to visit with me. Fan Club president Nona Lee Hayes was also a big supporter of mine, urging my appearances.

I remember one of those appearances. I was like a kid again; I went to the Opry and then came the sights and sounds of stars like Patsy Montana and Justin Tubb at the Jamboree. I stood backstage

David McCormick receives the IBMA Distinguished Achievement Award for Ernest Tubb Record Shops in 2008.

© 2008 Randall Franks Media – Randall Franks

and watched Patsy perform her song, "I Wanna Be A Cowboy's Sweetheart." Justin brought on several international artists on the show from Switzerland, Japan, and all over. The building overflowed with people, even though we were late because the Opry ran late. As I walked on the stage, my thoughts turned back to that star-struck kid who a few years before looked up from the audience at Ernest Tubb. That night, I thought, "I'm still that star-struck kid, just a little big-

ET Record Shop's Midnight Jamboree

ger." When I look at the stage, I see the one star performing. When I look from that stage, I see the true stars of the show — all of those in the audience who encourage with their smiles, applause, and cheers.

Ultimately, the person who placed their faith in me with the Midnight Jamboree was owner David McCormick. My latest projects have always made their way to fans through his stores.

I was honored to attend the International Bluegrass Music Association's World of Bluegrass Distinguished Achievement Awards when the Ernest Tubb Record Shop was honored. The award is the organization's second highest achievement, just below Hall of Fame induction. The honor comes because the stores have been marketing bluegrass music since the commercial inception, thus serving as one of the strongest advocates for the genre.

McCormick went to work with Ernest in the late 1960s when country music was just that, and Tubb eventually made him one of the co-owners. After the passing of Ernest and later the death of Justin, David has continued on as sole owner of the organization which has stores in Nashville, Pigeon Forge, and Texas.

The stores have become the place for true country music fans looking for those hard-to-find titles in country, bluegrass, and gospel. Every Saturday night, a list of stars hit the airwaves sharing their music and, of course, promoting the latest specials available either online at www.etrecordshop.com or in the stores.

The costs of sharing the Jamboree broadcast are making it more difficult for the store to produce new segments due to declining music sales. When it does air old or new shows, you may tune in online or radio and hear the broadcast. You can also listen to earlier broadcasts. I can never thank David enough for those opportunities that continue to this day as he shares my latest releases.

When I spoke to David, he was just thankful toward the artists who have graced the stage. As one of those artists, I think I can speak for all of us in saying we're the ones who are thankful for David's role in keeping the traditional music sounds alive and giving us all a place to hang our troubadour hats. Thanks also go out to Ernest and Justin.

© 1984 Randall Franks Media

Randall Franks performs for the Grand Ole Opry with his Peachtree Pickers in 1984.

Does Snake Oil Really Exist?

Do you have aches and pains? When you get up from the chair, does it take a few minutes for your body to catch up with you? Well step right up, and let me tell you about something that has been easing those problems for better than a century. Snake Oil, yes, famed in song and story and attributed by many as hokum. Snake Oil really does exist.

Is there snake in it?

Well, that's what some might think, but that name was originally chosen only to call attention to the product, according to the last real Snake Oil salesman in the world, "Doc" Tommy Scott (1917-2013) of Toccoa, Georgia.

Snake Oil comes in the form of a soothing rub-on liniment. For years, the memory of these purveyors of health and happiness from a

© 1999 Randall Franks Media

"Doc" Tommy Scott and Randall Franks at the Georgia Music Hall of Fame and Museum in 1999

Encouragers

bottle of herbs, roots and berries has been given a bad rap. The reputation largely came from shyster medicine men who would roll into town and sell some concoction cooked up in the back of the wagon which was promised to cure most any kind of ailment but in reality had little medicinal value.

In a memorable episode of the "Andy Griffith Show," such a character rolled into Mayberry, and the cure was mainly alcohol. Aunt Bee and all her friends, well, let's say, they got a bit tipsy.

In spite of the negative reputation given Snake Oil salesmen in films and popular culture, Scott continued to sell the recipe passed down from "Doc" Chamberlain who founded the medicine company and show in 1890 until his passing in 2013. Scott retired the Herb-O-Lac tonic laxative which once covered the South like molasses years earlier. While at one time the recipes were manufactured in the back of the wagon, the updated "S" Oil Liniment was prepared to meet Food and Drug Administration requirements.

While Scott has seen as many as 10,000 bottles a week of his tonic cures go out to happy customers, Scott believed in the power of the medicine by using it to ease his own aches and pains.

"A little rubbin' in the morning, another noon and night, you'll feel so well you'll want to yell, the stuff will make you right," Scott liked to share in his old-fashioned pitch.

He did believe that much of the power of any type of liniment is in the faith of the user.

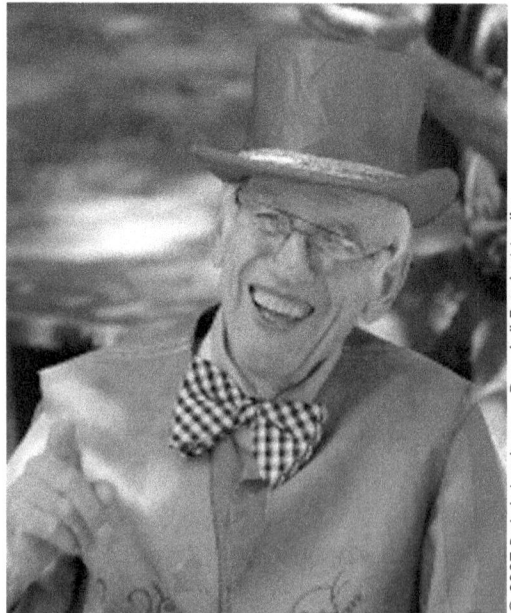

Tommy Scott relaxes between shows at Dayton, Tennessee, in 2007.

© 2007 Butch Lanham – Randall Franks Media

Does Snake Oil Really Exist?

As the aches and pains of cooler weather came in, orders for the mixture flooded his office in Toccoa. Folks of renown, including Oprah Winfrey and David Letterman, have opened up a bottle of the stuff. The Cincinnati Bengals at one time even credited it for helping their players through a winning season in 1986 while buying it by the case.

Whether it is through faith, or if there are truly benefits in herbal remedies, I do not know. The selling of herbal supplements has become a multimillion dollar industry. Instead of wagons, today they have infomercials, storefronts, and mail order catalogs.

Do the cures really work?

When I was faced with a particular discomforting childhood ailment, the doctors could not come up with anything to help me.

After my mother related the problem to my Grandma Kitty, she tucked her little burlap herb sack into the pocket of her apron and took to the woods to gather some of God's natural medicines. Before long, she was back with some odds and ends that a five-year-old would not likely go near. She ground up a mixture and gave it to me with more than some reluctance on my part. It worked. The doctors still did not believe it.

So, yes, I believe that there are many things in nature God put here to help us. When mixed in the right combination, I am sure they can relieve all types of discomforts. Unfortunately, unlike my grandmother, I do not know those combinations.

In regards to the mixture which is called Snake Oil, I've seen Snake Oil ease pains. Whether that is simply a matter of mind over matter, I do not know. I've heard many who would not let a winter go by without an ample supply on the shelf. I even keep a bottle with me everywhere I travel. You never know when a fiddler's fingers might need a little cooling off after playing a hot tune.

You may wonder why I consider this an encouraging element in my book. Well, the answer is two-fold. I have seen the power of encouragement this medicine had, and the man who sold it became one of the greatest encouragers of my life. Now, after its greatest salesman has moved his pitch box to a corner of a golden street in Heaven, requests still come in to his earthly office for the cure.

© 1984 Randall Franks Media

The Peachtree Pickers — 1984
From left are Mark Nelson (front), Lyndon Kolb,
Randall Franks, and Greg Earnest.

The "Green, Green Grass of Home"

Porter Wagoner

Wagoner

Porter Wagoner (1927–2007) became the favorite well-groomed, rhinestone-suited country crooner of millions of Americans through "The Porter Wagoner Show" that ran for twenty-one years on television and hit records. For fifty years, he was a member of the Grand Ole Opry cast.

I remember when I began working in Nashville years ago that the only star my Grandma Allie wanted a photo and autograph from was Porter.

I was privileged to meet Porter my first year in town. He was kind to me and many of the entertainers I worked with.

We often passed the time of day backstage at the Opry or at Opryland when it existed. I remember seeing him some years ago when he was serving as Opryland's Ambassador. His rhinestoned coats were left in the closet for rhinestone-covered Hawaiian-style shirts.

Several times, I appeared on Grand Master Fiddler Championship as a guest entertainer with Porter serving as host, and he also graciously allowed me to appear on his Grand Ole Opry show one time back in 1991.

Porter got his start on the farm in his home state of Missouri, rising from local radio to become part of the cast of the Ozark Jubilee.

Radio hits came slow for his own career, but he quickly gained success as a songwriter. Artist Carl Smith saw success with Porter's song, "Trademark."

Eventually his own performances, "Company's Comin' " (No. 7, 1954–1955) and "A Satisfied Mind" (No. 1, 1955) began climbing the charts, and he made the move to Nashville in 1956. In 1957, he joined the Opry. His fiftieth anniversary was celebrated earlier in 2007 with Dolly Parton singing the song she penned for him, "I Will Always Love You," on stage.

Porter helped to foster the careers of many performers, including Parton, Norma Jean, Buck Trent, Speck Rhodes, and others. Parton and he shared fourteen top ten hits. She visited him at the hospital in the last few days of his life, telling him that when he was better they'd do a duet on the Opry. She was with him and the family the day he died.

Porter won three Grammys ®, numerous country music awards, and according to his website, gained eighty-five chart hits in his career. "Misery Loves Company" (No. 1, 1962), "Green, Green Grass of Home" (No. 4, 1965), and "The Carroll County Accident" (No. 2, 1968–1969) are some of my favorites.

Despite suffering from a stomach aneurysm in 2006, he returned with a new release in 2007, "Wagonmaster," and heralded performances including New York's Madison Square Garden with the rock band White Stripes.

What can one say about the passing of one of America's most colorful entertainers?

It seemed that Porter would always be there — his smile, his suits shining in the lights, and his country charm that made you like him whether you were a fan of his music or not. Porter was bigger than country music itself. He was a star shining above a sea of performers. In fact, to many, he was the image of what country music should be.

If I had a coat like yours Porter, I would be holding it open, and sewn inside it would say "Wagonmaster, I'll see you when I reach the 'Green, Green Grass of Home.' May God bless you."

Fiddling Contests and The Grand Master Fiddler Championship

From our earliest days, we are encouraged to compete and succeed, whether through sports, scouting, or school.

As a Southern fiddler, your only route of competition was fiddling conventions or contests and the hope to one day go to the Grand Master Fiddler Championship.

As I was growing up, fiddling events were plentiful in the Southern region. In Georgia and Tennessee, they existed largely because the late mandolinist Bill Lowery of Chickamauga, Georgia, ramroded them into fruition.

Fiddling Contests and the Grand Master Fiddler

Lowery is a native of Sparta, Tennessee. He began playing at age twelve. His musical interests as a performer allowed him to appear on the Grand Ole Opry with Sam and Kirk McGee and Country Music Hall of Fame member Roy Acuff. He performed with Bluegrass Music Hall of Fame member Carl Story for ten months on television from Knoxville, Tennessee.

He was a guest artist on the Renfro Valley Barn Dance and participated in the Renfro Valley reunion show. He also played for two years on television for Johnnie Sue and Friends in the Chattanooga market. He performed internationally in Killarney, Ireland, appearing with two traditional Celtic bands. He is also known for his comedy and storytelling. He recorded five albums.

Randall Franks and Bill Lowery in 2012 visit at Lowery's induction at the Atlanta Country Music Hall of Honor.

As a mandolinist in contests, he won thirty-one major contests, including five Kentucky State Championships and four Southeastern USA events. One of his best-known contest tunes is "Twinkle Little Star." He composed the "Blue Mountain Waltz."

Over the years, he coordinated and served as emcee for over two hundred fiddler conventions in three states, including major events such as Stone Mountain's Yellow Daisy Festival, Dalton's Prater's Mill, Menlo's Fiddler's Contest, and other events throughout Georgia.

He was the coordinator of judges at the Tennessee Valley Fiddlers Convention in Athens, Alabama, for twenty years.

Lowery set the world record for the Guinness Book of World

Encouragers

Records in 1981 by playing six hundred twenty-three different tunes over thirty continuous hours of play.

He is an inductee in the North Georgia Musicians Hall of Fame and Atlanta Country Music Hall of Honor and is recognized in the White County Museum in Sparta, Tennessee.

From the point I was able to carry a decent tune, we were off and running to these events trying to gain a top spot, win some money, and in essence get the feedback we needed to improve.

A normal event required you to have at least six tunes under your belt: two breakdowns, two waltzes, and two tunes of choice. You needed three for eliminations and three generally for the finals.

Fiddlers gather at Lake Lanier Islands, Georgia, in 1994. From left, are Fletcher Bright, Dallas Burrell, Jack Weeks, and Roy Crawford.

It took me a long time to get my jitters to go away as I started this process, but eventually I was able to realize that much like a golfer, I was playing against myself. Yes, there were other fiddlers, but my goal was to be better than I was the last time.

However, I always dreaded knowing the end results.

Eventually, I would reach the goal, and start winning and taking home some money — of course, sharing some with my guitar player, who helped in the process. There were so many that helped out through the years, many from my band, but so many who just wanted to encourage me — Tom Adkins, Ray Brown, Clinton Carter, Chief Childers, and Al Smith, among others.

Fiddling and the Grand Master Fiddler

Through the years, I competed against some of the best contest fiddlers in the South. On some occasions, I was blessed to win or place, and sometimes I wasn't.

Some of my competitors were Jack Weeks, Wally Bryson, Roy Crawford, J.T. Perkins, John Henry Demps, Randy Howard, and Mark O'Connor.

Through the years, I won, placed, showed, and sometimes didn't come in at all.

Eventually, I gained the courage to go and compete at the Grand Master Fiddler Championship.

Perry Harris

© Dean Tokuno

The Grand Master Fiddler Championship was the brainchild of the late Perry F. Harris, M.D., D.D.S., who organized the event with the support of Roy Acuff, E.W. "Bud" Wendell, Porter Wagoner, WSM, the Grand Ole Opry, the Country Music Association, and many other country music personalities.

It continues today under the guidance of Perry's son Howard Harris, fiddler Ed Carnes, and a great board of directors for the Tennessee non-profit corporation, the Grand Master Fiddler Championship, Inc. I am honored to serve the organization as its host each year for the two-day event now associated with the Country Music Hall of Fame.

"The purpose of

Ed Carnes (left) and Howard Harris present the Dr. Perry F. Harris Award to Dolly Parton in 2010.

© 2009 Grand Master Fiddler

Randall Franks plays at
the Ryman Auditorium with Eugene Akers
backing him on guitar.

Fiddling Contests and the Grand Master Fiddler

the Grand Master Fiddler Championship is not only to recognize the top fiddle player in North America or even the world; but to also educate and perpetuate fiddling as an art form and cultural treasure," said Howard Harris,

Randall Franks entertains at the Grand Master Fiddler Championship in 1994.

chairman and CEO. "Our status as a nonprofit corporation ensures that the competitive and educational aspects we support will be tied solely to the nonprofit corporation and not to commercial interests."

For more than three decades, the event brought together the finest

Benny Martin

players from around the world with entertainment from the biggest stars of country music.

When I became associated with the event, the Championship was held in the historic Ryman Auditorium and Opryland USA theme park. It ended in 1997. Some of my favorite memories reach back to this event and the people who became part of my musical family through it — Howdy Forrester, Curly Fox, the Bush family of Charlie and

Encouragers

Sam, Wild Bill Lyell, Benny Martin, George Custer, Mark O'Connor, and Alison Krauss. The list goes on and on.

Randall Franks hosts the Grand Master Fiddler Championship in 2012.

The eliminations were held at the Ryman Auditorium where the fiddler found in front of him a light akin to a traffic signal giving him the time limit of his playing. If he played into the red, it counted against him.

I remember being scared to death, and while the tunes I fit in my six minutes are a distant memory, I know the judges could hear my nerves were rattled. Among them were them Howdy Forrester and Benny Martin.

As a result of the event, I spent a lifetime lost in the Opryland Hotel one time. In one of my comedy routines, "Big Tige, Mr. Roy and Me," I share my experience of being lost with legend Roy Acuff and Benny Martin as we wander through this adventure looking for the fiddler's party following the competition. I recall my first time sitting and listening to the amazing talents of Sam Bush, with whom years later we'd share a featured appearance in one of Dolly Parton's movies, "Blue Valley Songbird." My first acquaintances with Grand Ole Opry stars The Whites, now of "O Brother Where Art Thou" fame, and dobroist Jerry Douglas, who would both later record with me, began long friendships during this time.

Standing in the alley outside the Ryman Auditorium, I first met Alison Krauss as we rehearsed and waited our turns to compete in the preliminaries and hoped we were passed into the finals. Alas, neither of us was, but it gave me some wonderful comedy material years later

Fiddling Contests and the Grand Master Fiddler

as I hosted the Bluegrass Music Awards and presented her with one of her many awards.

As my star continued to rise and I no longer competed, Dr. Harris was a tremendous supporter of mine behind the scenes at the Grand Ole

© 1994 Randall Franks Media

Jack Weeks and Randall Franks at the 1994 Southeastern Invitational

Opry. Whenever possible, I would schedule to appear as one of the stars who entertained the audiences at the competition.

Today, I am honored to serve as celebrity host for the event as Roy Acuff and Porter Wagoner did in the past. For more information, visit GrandMasterFiddler.com.

Because of the influence these contests had on my life beginning in 1994, I agreed to host the Georgia state-sponsored Fiddlin' Fish Arts and Crafts Festival Randall Franks Southeastern Fiddle-Off.

The winner took away the Randall Franks Trophy along with a cash prize and a new violin. Of course, Dr. Harris helped me with it by coming to judge, and the winner was invited to compete in the finals of the Grand

© 2011 Randall Franks Media

Johnny Ray Watts competes for the Randall Franks Trophy in 2011.

71

Encouragers

Master Fiddler.

I was extremely honored when the fiddler I had lost to more times than I could count won — Jack Weeks. In all the years of competing against him, I had only won against Jack one time.

The state presented this for two years. The Randall Franks Trophy returned at the 1890s Day Jamboree Old Time Fiddle Convention in Ringgold, Georgia, with its first presentation in 2006 going to another fiddler I once competed against — Johnny Ray Watts. He has won the trophy on three occasions.

As of 2014, I have awarded eleven Randall Franks Trophy winners.

Randall Franks Trophy Winners

Fiddlin' Fish Arts and Crafts Festival
Randall Franks Southeastern Fiddle-Off
Lake Lanier Islands, Ga.
1994 Jack Weeks *Dalton, Georgia*
1995 Roy Crawford *Cullman, Alabama*

1890s Day Jamboree Old Time Fiddlers Convention
Ringgold, Ga.
2006 Johnny Ray Watts *Lineville, Alabama*
2007 Aerin DeJarnette *Snellville, Georgia*
2008 Mark Ralph *Huntsville, Alabama*
2009 Doug Fleener *Leitchfield, Kentucky*
2010 Megan Lynch *Goodlettsville, Tennessee*
2011 Johnny Ray Watts *Lineville, Alabama*
2012 Johnny Ray Watts *Lineville, Alabama*
2013 Maddie Denton *Murfreesboro, Tennessee*
2014 Maddie Denton *Murfreesboro, Tennessee*

Bill Anderson

Our parents often help form our tastes in music, movies, and the like. For me, one of those parental favorites from my mom was Whisperin' Bill Anderson.

Georgia-raised Country Music and Georgia Music Hall of Fame member Bill Anderson has more than eighty hits to his personal credit.

Anderson's career has spanned more than fifty years and provided listeners

Bill Anderson visits with Pearl Franks in 1992.

© 1992 Randall Franks Media — Donna Tracy

with countless hits both as an artist and as a songwriter. I have known Bill since I was a youngster dreaming of someday being a performer. At each of our visits through the years, he has always been sincerely interested in what I was doing. I have watched him share the same interest in the fans.

Bill began his musical career as a disc jockey at WJJC in Commerce, Georgia, and was a sports writer for the DeKalb News Era.

Countless hits have come from his pen since his "City Lights" went to number one for Ray Price in 1958. Some of his personal hits include "Still," "Po Folks," and "Mama Sang a Song." In recent years, he has written or co-written hits for Vince Gill, Kenny Chesney, Mark Wills, Brad Paisley, Alison Krauss, and George Strait. Anderson, who continues to star on the Grand Ole Opry, also appeared on the soap opera One Life to Live and hosted network game shows.

Once his hits began, he just kept them coming with thirty-seven top ten singles and scores of hits for artists from Ray Price to Conway Twitty, according to a Hall of Fame article by Walt Trott.

He has hosted television shows and was the longtime host of the Georgia Music Hall of Fame Awards.

To learn more about Bill Anderson visit www.billanderson.com.

Randall Franks — 1987

"Catfish John" and "Jesse Taylor"

"Act Naturally" was a song written by a mild-mannered songwriter named Johnny Russell (1940-2001). The Beatles and Buck Owens and so many more sang it. For most of my life, Johnny was a regular at the Grand Ole Opry. His ability to entertain an audience made him a favorite.

Johnny carried quite a few pounds with him on stage. He would come out and say, "Can everybody see me all right?" His ability to bring down the house with his low-key, easy-going humor always kept me interested in seeing what he would do or say next.

Through the years, I had many opportunities to work with this song-smith. He not only co-wrote "Act Naturally" with Voni Morrison, which was the flipside of the Beatles' 1965 multi-million selling

Johnny Russell and Randall Franks serve up some food to the fans at the Ernest Tubb Record Shop's Fan Appreciation Day in Nashville, Tennessee.

Encouragers

"Yesterday" single, at the age of nineteen, his "In a Mansion Stands My Love," was chosen by Chet Atkins to be included in a 1959 Jim Reeves recording session. The song became the flip side of the million seller "He'll Have To Go." Other notable compositions include "Making Plans" by Porter Wagoner and Dolly Parton, which reached number two in 1980; "Let's Fall To Pieces Together" by George Strait, which reached number one in 1984; and "You'll Be Back (Every Night In My Dreams)" by the Statlers, which reached number three in 1982. These were just a few of the songs.

As an artist, he had twenty-eight Billboard chart songs. In 1973, the songs "Catfish John," which reached number twelve; and "The Baptism of Jesse Taylor," which reached number fourteen; still ring in my childhood memories as these characters' stories struck my imagination. His biggest hit came from a song he did not write when "Rednecks, White Socks and Blue Ribbon Beer" went to number four in 1973.

I greatly admired Johnny's ability to make an audience happy. Of all the performers with whom I shared the bill, he was one I always hoped I would not have to follow on stage.

He left the audience wanting more. While I never told him, that is something I learned from him, and as a result I carry a little bit of him with me each time I walk on stage. Mr. Russell, thanks for making me laugh and letting me learn by just being around you.

Yea, though I walk through the valley of the shadow of death, I will fear no evil: for thou art with me; thy rod and thy staff they comfort me.

Psalm 23:4

The Whites — Always on the Sunny Side

I leaned against the wall of the Nashville Convention Center a few feet from the stage in October 2006. Tears rolled down my cheeks as I saw Emmylou Harris present three of the most wonderful people I have ever met with the International Bluegrass Music Association's Distinguished Achievement Award.

This honor is given to those proven to be forerunners in their particular field of endeavor and/or who fostered bluegrass music's image with developments that will broaden the music's recognition and accessibility.

It stands second only to induction into the Hall of Honor as the industry's greatest accolade.

Grand Ole Opry stars The Whites certainly are deserving of this honor, and they were in fine company as they joined several other friends — the Boys from Indiana, Bill Grant, and Ronnie Reno. Fred Bartenstein was also honored.

I have had the pleasure of knowing The Whites — Buck, Cheryl, Sharon, and Rosie — for more years than either of us care to count. I met them originally through their appearances for the Grand Masters Fiddle Championship. Buck and his late wife Pat were big fans of fiddling, and I remember spending endless hours sitting with Pat in the stands watching the competition and talking. Pat was a wonderful spirit who brought light and hope into her conversations with others, including me.

The family began their adventure in Buck's home state of Texas, relocated to Arkansas, and in the early seventies made Nashville their home. They gained nationwide recognition in the late seventies through recording with

Randall Franks, Pat White, and Eugene Akers at Country Music Fan Fair in 1983

© 1983 Randall Franks Music – Jean Osborn

Encouragers

The Whites continue to keep the tradition in country music in this performance for the
Grand Master Fiddler Championship in 2010.

Emmylou Harris on "Blue Kentucky Girl" and then serving as her opening act.

It wasn't long before they became shining country stars themselves, landing several top ten hits of the 1980s, including "You Put the Blue in Me," "Hangin' Around," "Give Me Back That Old Familiar Feeling," and "Pins And Needles."

They joined the Grand Ole Opry in 1984. Buck told me in an interview that this for him was the group's greatest achievement.

"Getting on the Grand Ole Opry was something I dreamed of for years," he said. "I never thought I'd be there to be a member."

He said that while the music is changing by being louder and featuring more drums and electric guitars, their group is still bringing its traditional sound to the mix.

"The people my age still like the fiddles," he said.

The Whites' performance of "Keep on the Sunny Side" in "O Brother Where Art Thou" won them a Grammy ® and made me

The Whites — Always on the Sunny Side

proud.

Sharon White Skaggs, wife of Ricky Skaggs, shared with me that the movie really changed the direction of their performance career and put them back on the road in full force. Buck said that the movie experience allowed them to see all the venues they played filled.

"It was the music that made the movie," he said. "It really did give a shot in the arm to hillbilly and old country music."

Buck said that receiving the Distinguished Achievement Award was quite unexpected.

"As I said at the event, there are those who are more deserving but not anybody more appreciative," he said. "It's good to be recognized."

As they lingered in the hall following the event, dozens of people stopped by to share with them a favorite memory. While I visited with each member of the family, I enjoyed standing quietly and hearing the immenseness of the love being shared in both directions from the fans to The Whites, and especially from The Whites to their fans. I know that they all made a special effort to make me feel at home in an environment from which I had been absent for quite a while and

© 1991 Randall Franks Media – Ben Hall

Sharon, Cheryl, and Buck of The Whites, and Randall Franks visit in the Homeplace studio after recording "Let's Live Everyday Like It Was Christmas" in 1991.

The Whites and Jerry Douglas perform on the IBMA
Awards in Nashville, Tennessee, in 2010.

offered counsel in the loss of my mother.

"We've always tried to be influences toward the good side of
life," Buck said. "Be helpful, give of your time and talents."

While much of the shape of country music is shifting to a more
worldly look and sound, The Whites remain a constant beacon of
hope in the rough waves filled with country pretenders.

Their musical career has brought endless hours of joy to millions
of fans around the world. For me, their friendship has always brought
knowledge that if I was in trouble, I had someone upon whom I could
call. As Pat or Buck would quickly remind me, I can always call on
God because, "It's not what you know, it's Who you know."

*Comfort ye, comfort ye my people,
saith your God.*

Isaiah 40:1

Stunning Stella

Stella Parton and Randall Franks take direction from Eric Straton on the set of "Phoenix Falling" in 1997.

When you look at Americans who have made a difference in people's lives through their careers and their daily work, one who comes to mind is entertainer Stella Parton.

One of my favorite experiences was getting to co-star with her in the film "Phoenix Falling." Our film characters were an interesting mixture of her charm and refinement and my rather staggering stupor as an outer space architect who relied more on the bottle than on his abilities. While filming on location, I had the opportunity to spend some quality time with this lady, and let me tell you she is one of the nicest individuals I have ever met.

Throughout our years of association, she has always been a source of encouragement, guidance, advice, and friendship. She was even kind enough to share her time for our scholarship foundation in Ringgold named for my late parents.

Since her first hit single, "I Want to Hold You in My Dreams Tonight," through twenty-six albums and over two dozen chart singles, plus numerous awards and nominations, Stella has touched millions.

With her unique ability to relate with people in all walks of life, she devotes herself to special causes such as domestic violence. She helps women build self-esteem by sharing her knowledge of hair and makeup at the New Opportunity School for Women in Berea, Kentucky.

She donned a cap and gown to accept her certification from the American Association of Christian Counselors.

In addition, when performing across the United States, Stella donates a portion of her cookbook sales to the domestic violence shelter in the particular city she is in.

She features her life experiences in an uplifting book. "The title is 'Tell It Sister, Tell It: Memories, Music and Miracles.' It has got a lot of my humor. It is very inspirational and very Christian, but at the same time, it has secular slang in it. I don't want to change it because I feel like I walked that ground. I am not so churchified that I can't say 'poop' with a mouth full. But I will be the first one to pray for you if you need praying for."

Stella Parton performs for the Share America Foundation in 2009.

© 2009 Randall Franks Media – Randall Franks

As a stage, film, and television actress, Stella has starred in numerous projects. Her works include "Seven Brides for Seven Brothers," "Gentlemen Prefer Blondes," and "Cloud Dancer." She is also a talented chef and cookbook author.

While musing about her years of success in a variety of areas, she said, "It is just a business. If you've been lucky enough to make a living, you just hang right in there."

For more information about Stella Parton, visit her website at www.stellaparton.com.

The Fabulous Ferlin Husky

One of my favorite all time songs is "Wings of a Dove." I also have tremendous admiration for the artist who made the song possible — Ferlin Husky (1925–2011).

I had the honor of meeting Ferlin some years ago in Branson when I came in to make an appearance for the Ernest Tubb Record Shop. That day there was a gathering, a who's who if you will, of country's favorites who called Branson their performance home — Boxcar Willie, Ferlin, and Jim Owens, among others.

I enjoyed a nice visit with Ferlin in July 2008 and had the chance to speak with him from his home in Missouri by telephone.

Even in his eighties, he still enjoyed performing and singing. He sold more than twenty million records. Among his hits are "Gone," "Wings of a Dove," "A Dear John Letter," and "Country Music is Here to Stay," performed by his alter-ego Simon Crum.

Ferlin recalled that he and musician/writer Bob Ferguson wrote "Wings of a Dove" together, although he let Ferguson have all the writer's credits because Ferlin published the song.

"It took me five years to get it recorded," he said. "Mr. Ken Nelson, A and R Man at Capitol (Records) in Nashville, said people are not buying those religious type songs. It won't sell.

"Every time I'd record, I'd bring it up," he said. "Finally he said to me one day, 'You keep talking about that song. If you want to. Do it, but you will be history.'"

Husky gave up the notion and went on to try to get others to record it, for some time to avail. Finally, five years later, he was able to slip it into a session when a missed plane connection kept Nelson from a session.

The song was released as the B-side of what Nelson felt was the hit "Next to Jimmy," but the B-side prevailed.

When it came to his hit "Gone," Ferlin put his own special stamp on the song as he envisioned an old time gospel sound on the song.

Using the Jordanaires and Millie Kirkham along with the musicians, the studio quickly filled.

Nelson warned Ferlin, "'You're out of your mind. If one more person walks in, the session is off.'"

Encouragers

Even though it was his second try at recording "Gone" (He first recorded it under the name Terry Preston with the Cliffie Stone Band.), this time he was determined to do it his way. He did and made the song hit.

Ferlin had the attention of the television leaders throughout his career. He often appeared on the biggest shows of the day, including those of Ed Sullivan, Steve Allen, Mike Douglas, Merv Griffin, and Dean Martin as well as the Tonight Show with Johnny Carson. He even replaced Arthur Godfrey on his show in 1957.

"I had an eighth-grade education. Someone from the country where I was raised on the farm and get to replace the man that was the giant in television — known as one of best pitch men in business," he said. "Of all the announcers, for them to pick me to do his summer replacement in 1957."

He also appeared in about eighteen films and serials like the "Durango Kid" during his time on the west coast.

Husky said his life allowed him to fulfill all the dreams he imagined as a boy on the farm near Flat River, Missouri.

"I have been blessed. God's been awful good to me," he said.

Who comforteth us in all our tribulation, that we may be able to comfort them which are in any trouble, by the comfort wherewith we ourselves are comforted of God.

2 Corinthians 1:4

Pickin' and Grinnin' Friends
Bluegrass Music

Margie and Enoch Sullivan
of The Sullivan Family — 1988

*"Margie and Enoch Sullivan were the first
promoters to book me to perform
a show in Nashville in 1983."*
Randall Franks

Bill Monroe — Stepping into Kenny Baker's Shoes

My first close association with Bill Monroe (1911–1996) came after leaving the stage following playing with Josh Graves in 1983 at the Jekyll Island Bluegrass Festival. After a short, dressing room jam session that included several musicians, everyone went on their way except Mr. Monroe and I. He initially asked me if I knew how to play "Katy Hill," and from there began a three-hour, one-on-one fiddle lesson with the man himself.

Randall Franks and Bill Monroe visit backstage at Jekyll Island, Georgia, in 1989 in the room where they shared their first teaching session in 1983.

We started a friendship that day, and I was soon invited to visit him on his farm in Nashville. I had the honor of helping with the creation of the Bill Monroe Bluegrass Hall of Fame and worked with Pete Kuykendall and others in the process.

I made my first appearances with Bill Monroe the summer of 1984, initially at Fan Fair, then at Dahlonega Bluegrass Festival, and later in Nashville at the opening of the Hall of Fame.

After the departure of Kenny Baker, Monroe's fiddler for more than twenty-two years, Mr. Monroe was searching for the person that he wanted to mold to fit the tremendous void left by Baker's departure. I was honored that he gave me the chance. When the opening came, it was Sue Lewis, wife of Blue Grass Boy Wayne Lewis, and Betty McInturff, his long time personal assistant, who helped facilitate Mr. Monroe in hiring me for the job while he was occupied with

Encouragers

a tour of Japan.

Still in my teens, I was in school and managed to convince my professors that this was an opportunity of a lifetime. I'm thankful they agreed and allowed me to miss classes, do my schoolwork on the road, and return for the mid-term

Randall Franks and Wayne Lewis

and final exams. While the plan worked that quarter, it was doubtful that it was something that I could sell to the next group of professors. A choice would have to be made as to whether to continue in college or perform with the Blue Grass Boys.

Of course, it is obvious what my youthful choice would have been. There was no greater role to fill as a fiddler than to be Bill Monroe's fiddler, and there I was.

I officially put on the hat in Yakima, Washington, in late October 1984 and stayed with the Blue Grass Boys for appearances in several states as we crossed the country playing fiddle and bass, alternating with Tater Tate.

At a performance at Myrtle Beach, South Carolina, my parents, Floyd and Pearl, came to see me perform with Mr. Monroe. They had seen me before appearing as a guest at the Grand Ole Opry Show at Fan Fair and at Mountain Music Park in Dahlonega, Georgia, but not since I officially became part of the band. Mr. Bill and they went out to dinner together, and it was around that dinner table that my future was decided.

This experience was related to me long after my work with Bill Monroe. Had I known of the arrangement then in my headstrong youth, it may have formed a different destiny for me.

My parents had managed my entertainment career since I began touring, so this actually was not that unusual. They were well set in

Bill Monroe — Stepping into Kenny Baker's Shoes

their direction for my life. I was the first in my family to attend college, and they wanted me to finish; to have a solid future in the event my childhood entertainment success did not carry through into adulthood as happens for so many performers.

Mr. Monroe wanted me to come to work for him so that he could work with me more closely and mold me to do what he believed he needed to fill the fiddle role in the Blue Grass Boys.

They came to the agreement that I would continue my college career and fill in for Bill whenever he was in a tight and it did not conflict with school.

I didn't know the content of this agreement until my mother told me years later what he had done for me. I do recall him telling her one time backstage at the Opry: "We did a good job didn't we? He got a good education."

I made my final official appearance wearing the hat in 1985 in Sparta, Tennessee, at the High School Auditorium.

Mr. Monroe knew he had the strength to pull me in and keep me with the Blue Grass Boys with the weight of simply asking, yet he respected my parents' wishes and let me return to school and continued his search.

Without knowing this arrangement, I was a bit dismayed at the time wondering whether my insufficiencies as a musician kept me from continuing in the band.

Of course, when people asked about my departure, I replied that I had to get back to school.

While I never did return to the Blue Grass Boys, he often featured me as a guest on his show and facilitated many of the opportunities for me to appear for the Grand Ole Opry with whichever musical configuration I was promoting at the time.

He was always cheering me on in my career accomplishments. I always looked to him for advice and his encouragement.

In one of the last conversations we had before his passing he said to me, "I tell you man, folks like you and me have got to stick together and be friends with one another. There aren't that many folks today like us that you can depend upon."

© 1984 Randall Franks Media

Randall Franks — 1984

Bill Monroe — Don't Cry in Your Crush

Spending most of my life on the road as a performer, I have become very accustomed to the rigors of traveling. One thing you tolerate but never get adjusted to are the close quarters you and up to five or six other musicians share while on the road. It takes a tremendous amount of respect and consideration for people to make such a situation livable, especially if you are not related.

Course, if you are related, it probably takes more.

If you are blessed with the benefit of traveling by bus, you at least have the luxury of getting up and walking the aisles from time to time. You almost get a rhythm of knowing how to shift your weight to keep from falling down. You do, however, have to make your departure from the bus known. If you happen to get off at a 76 truck stop in rural Idaho at 2 a.m. to get a bottle of pop, you may be crying in your grape Crush when you see those taillights in the distance and you're standing there in your sock feet.

A view from the front of Bill Monroe's bus in 1984

© 1984 Randall Franks Media – Randall Franks

While working with Bill Monroe and his Blue Grass Boys, I believe I learned every way to sleep on a moving bus — standing up, sitting down, lying down, and standing on my head. One way I never tried was related to me during my tenure with the multi-award win-

91

Encouragers

ning southern gospel quartet The Marksmen Quartet. One of their early members would sleep face down in the bunk — arms folded, head on arms, face down in the bunk.

Why?

He would fix his hair before leaving for the weekend. Then he would sleep that way to keep his hair looking just right. Apparently, it works.

Late at night while traveling with Monroe, I would walk down the aisle and sit down on the carpeted step as he rode shotgun in the jumper seat which folded out in the door opening. He would often reminisce about his sixty years of traveling, or he would sit quietly in his La-Z-Boy recliner, and we would pass the miles by playing gin rummy. He was hard to beat, but I did a time or two.

No matter whom you travel with, if you spend enough time together, eventually you will feel the sting of a practical joke.

Now, I'm not talking about anything mean or malicious, just friendly little jokes that did not hurt anyone.

While traveling with Monroe, our lead singer, Wayne Lewis, was what you might call a bit jumpy. He didn't like folks coming up and surprising him from behind. One time, when we played Fort Collins, Colorado, we stayed in adjacent rooms on about the eighth floor. Since it was a warm winter's day, the windows were open. There was about a twenty-inch ledge outside the two open windows, and in my youthful fervor, I decided to step out and try to startle him through the open window. Conveniently, he had his back to the window. When I stood outside his window and said "Boo!," he almost jumped out of his skin.

Of course, he got me back.

While traveling with the Marksmen, sometimes we traveled by bus, sometimes by van with a trailer.

Traveling by van with five or six people is just like AT&T — you can reach out and touch someone whether you want to or not. Like the bus, the van was converted with four sleeping bunks. One time I crawled up in the bunk to get a little sleep while we were traveling. I think it was to a little town in Texas. In this case, I was in a top bunk.

Bill Monroe — Don't Cry in Your Crush

It was sort of like crawling up into a well-upholstered sardine can with about ten inches between you and the ceiling. You could not sit up; you just had to roll off. Despite the tight space, it was very comfortable. While I was out of it, my compadres quietly had something up their sleeves. It wasn't the conventional shaving cream in the shoe kind of thing either. This took some pre-planning on someone's part.

While I was sleeping soundly, we arrived at the venue grounds.

When I awoke, I found myself tied with a rope to the bunk from head to toe. I could not have moved if I wanted too. And let me just say I did want too; it had been a long trip. There wasn't a soul around. I had hoped to free myself with a Buck hunting knife kept under the pillow, but unfortunately, the trusted knife had cut out on me too.

One night as I sat on the step of Bill Monroe's old blue tour bus watching the gray hills of Washington go by, the rain beat heavily upon the front windshield giving an almost rhythmic cadence to its fall.

As Bill Monroe sat in the door seat hovering above the steps, he stared off into the distance, seemingly in deep meditation.

As he, the driver, and I stared down the highway, from Bill's lips came the words "Farther along we'll know all about it; Farther along we'll understand why; Cheer up my brother, live in the sunshine; We'll understand it all by and by."

We joined in humming with him in harmony as the rain kept perfect rhythm behind our offering.

When Bill stopped singing he turned to me and asked, "Did I ever tell you about the time I almost died in a car accident?"

I said "No." He got quiet again, and in a few minutes he said, "I'll tell you man it took a powerful strong hand to get me through it." He said that he was going fox hunting back up in Kentucky in early 1953 and he had put the dogs in the trunk. It seems like he told me the road and town, but the memory has faded.

As I recall, on one of those desolate back roads, a car crossed the center lane and hit Bill head-on, throwing him from the vehicle and leaving him lying on the side of the road unconscious. What struck me more than the accident was the strong memory that he still carried from after the accident.

As he lay there on the side of the road broken and bleeding, what he remembered most was when someone stopped after the accident. Still in his state of dazed unconsciousness, he recalls the person trying to pull the rings from his fingers rather than trying to help him.

By the time real help finally arrived, Bill was coming around and refused to be carried into the hospital and said he walked in on his own speed — a great feat considering all the fractures he told me that his body sustained. While I wish I could recall more of the details of the story, alas, it is gone with time; but I do know that the incident put Bill off the road and out of recording for most of that year. By the way, the dogs survived without a scratch, he said.

And after the reading of the law and the prophets the rulers of the synagogue sent unto them, saying, Ye men and brethren, if ye have any word of exhortation for the people, say on.

Acts 13:15

A Moment with Doc Watson and Bill Monroe

© Courtesy Violet Hensley

Watson

As I stepped into the dingy white dressing room with tongue and groove walls, I noticed him sitting over in the corner with his guitar in his hand, tuning up his B string.

I stood in awe of this man's unique ability to wrap himself around any song and make it his own.

He was blind, and though I never had spent much time around anyone without sight, I felt it appropriate to walk over and introduce myself.

"Mr. Watson, I am Randall Franks," I said.

He raised his head towards me and stuck out his hand.

"I am here working with Jim and Jesse," I said.

When you step up onto a tour bus, you sometimes do not know the specifics about your destination or with whom you will be working until you arrive.

Jim and Jesse made me a regular guest star on the Jim and Jesse Show, and I always enjoyed having the opportunity to travel with these bluegrass legends.

This weekend included three stops in different towns.

I appeared on the same festivals with Doc Watson (1923–2012) and his late son Merle in the past, and although I met Merle, who died tragically in a tractor accident in 1985, I had never had a chance to really meet Doc. The multi-Grammy winning artist was doing what he loved, sitting in a corner of a back room in an auditorium.

Doc Watson is one of traditional music's greatest influencers, bursting onto the scene during the folk revival of the 1960s. With the folk revival waning, he struck gold again as part of the original Nitty Gritty Dirt Band "Will the Circle Be Unbroken" album cast. One of my favorite albums featured a combination of Doc, Lester Flatt, and Earl Scruggs.

While his style and mine were different, I was anxious to soak in a bit of what he did.

We passed a few pleasantries as I got my fiddle out and tuned it up. He was singing a bit of "Riding that Midnight Train" when another icon walked backstage — Bill Monroe with his mandolin in hand.

Encouragers

He took out his Gibson F-5, turned a couple of keys, and joined right in.

While I already was a former Blue Grass Boy, as these two great voices melded on traditional songs such as "What Would You Give in Exchange for Your Soul" and "Banks of the Ohio," the hair on the back of my neck stood up.

Here I was with my fiddle in hand, throwing in a bit and a piece with these two innovators.

As we played a little "Fire on the Mountain," I envisioned myself on stage with these two icons at the Newport Folk Festival in 1963 when they took the audience by storm together.

As the stage show went on outside, I thought to myself that the show was really going on right here. This was a solid gold performance that happened totally by accident.

Sadly, it came and went without notice of anyone except us three.

I can tell you though, as someone sitting on the front row, I wish you were there to feel the combination of Watson's guitar style and Monroe's mandolin. I believe that the sound beckoned back to the 1930s Monroe Brothers that took the Carolinas by storm and set brother Bill on his path to forge the new genre of bluegrass.

Whom I have sent unto you for the same purpose, that he might know your estate, and comfort your hearts;

Colossians 4:8

Jim and Jesse — A Sound Unequaled

Jim (right) and Jesse McReynolds prepare to tape a commercial for WCYB-TV NBC in Bristol, Virginia in 1993.

It has been a long time since I was a star-struck boy sitting in front of the stage at the Lavonia Bluegrass Festival in Lavonia, Georgia. It was there that I first saw in person a pair of performers who for me, on recordings and radio, set the standard for quality and class in music.

I sat in awe as Grand Ole Opry stars Jim and Jesse and the Virginia Boys rolled out "Cotton Mill Man," "Johnny B. Goode," "Paradise," "Diesel On My Tail" and countless other songs and tunes. The combination of the brother duet's artistry, the steady guitar work by Jim, and the virtuosity of Jesse's mandolin playing created a sound that has not been equaled.

It amazed me how Jim McReynolds (1927–2002) just opened up his mouth and the smoothest, purest tenor flowed trippingly off his tongue. One could only aspire to sing like he did.

His quiet presence in any situation brought an air of dignity. It was like when Billy Graham walks into a room — you just knew what kind of man he was and with whom he walked.

My father Floyd first struck up a relationship with Jim and Jesse so many years ago at Lavonia. Where I was not very talkative, dad could always find something to say.

Encouragers

That was the beginning, but later Eugene Akers helped me build upon that, and ultimately Jean Osborn placed me working with their fan club so that I became part of the Jim and Jesse family. Jean was one of country music's longest running fan club presidents and as such had earned a tremendous amount of respect in the industry. She opened so many doors for me with just a good word about what I was doing.

Working with president Jean Osborn, I helped promote Jim and Jesse in any way I could by becoming the publicity arm of the organization on its twenty-fifth anniversary in the eighties.

Jesse once described the relationship that our families shared together as one big family — for years we all got together and spent days on end working together — laughing and sharing with those who loved the music.

It is safe to say that of all the professional perform-

Jim and Jesse McReynolds and Mac Wiseman work in the studio with producer Randall Franks in 1991.

© 1991 Randall Franks Media – Donna Tracy

ers with whom I have spent time, none have inspired me, counseled me, and guided me more than Jim McReynolds and Jesse McReynolds.

As my star began to rise, Jim and Jesse helped to elevate my stature in the industry by taking me under their wings.

I began promoting concerts with Jim, Jesse, myself, and other acts. Jim and Jesse would also include me as part of their show on countless other performances across the country. When I made national television appearances, I would ask Jim and Jesse and the

Jim and Jesse — A Sound Unequaled

Virginia Boys to assist me, and they graciously would. Even when I made appearances for the Grand Ole Opry, they would step out to support me musically, serving as my band as I entertained audiences.

One of my greatest memories is when I arranged for Jim and Jesse to introduce "In the Heat of the Night" stars Alan Autry, "Bubba," and David Hart, "Parker," and me to the Opry stage in 1991. I had the pleasure that night of being a Virginia Boy on the Grand Ole Opry and supported them for a change by playing twin fiddle on "I'll Never Love Anybody But You."

Jim McReynolds

As I came to know both of the brothers, my relationship with each was different. With Jim, initially we found common ground in the business of the industry.

I spent endless hours traveling across the country on Jim and Jesse's bus. They would often pull off I-75 and pick me up in Tunnel Hill.

As Jim drove, he and I would wile away the hours talking about politics, religion, prob-

Jim and Jesse McReynolds and Randall Franks pause for media after leaving the Grand Ole Opry's Fan Fair stage in 1992. Jim and Jesse and the Virginia Boys were Randall's band at this event.

© 1992 Randall Franks Media – Donna Tracy

lems in the music industry, and our hopes for the future. Jim was one to stay with the tried and true. If it worked, he did not see much need to change. One thing about it — Jim and Jesse worked.

Encouragers

I would say Jim was the traditionalist of the duo. He preferred to stay with successful approach and keep working. He made the steady guitar work he did seem as effortless as his crystal clear tenor. Jim had a great sense of humor that over the years seemed to come out more and more on stage despite his attempts to maintain a reserved nature.

Through the years, I would often call Jim and his wife Arreta would call to him, pulling him off the tractor. We would catch up, sometimes setting up a performance somewhere or discussing whatever the latest topic of interest was in music city. We even managed to continue this as he battled thyroid cancer. In our last conversation, we promised we'd talk again.

Their daughter, Janeen, became like a sister to me as we spent hours working and traveling together as I toured with the Jim and Jesse Show or worked on some project that we were all involved in.

Randall Franks visits with Janeen McReynolds-Reynolds (right) and Gwen McReynolds (left), who is holding Jim's grandson James at the Pick Inn in 2008.

When Alan and I were developing a new television series idea based on his "Mean Joe Blake" film script, we tapped Jim and Jesse to help with the series' theme music. I can still hear the clear echo of Jim's tenor ringing out "Mean Joe." If our series had been successful, all of America could have heard their artistry every week.

Jesse described Jim's talents in this way:

"Jim had his own sound, his own way of singing," he said. "He was one of a kind. We tried to create our own sound and put good

Jim and Jesse — A Sound Unequaled

musicians with it to try to capture that sound. We would like for it to be remembered as the Jim and Jesse sound of bluegrass."

© 2008 Randall Franks Media

Jesse McReynolds

Randall Franks (left) performs with Jesse and Garrett McReynolds in Gallatin, Tennessee, in 2008.

With Jesse, our common ground was the creativeness of music itself, and finding new approaches to the innovation of the sound, the business, and ultimately both our careers.

Jesse and his wife, Darlene, were blessed with several children

© 2001 Randall Franks Media

Randall Franks and Luke McKnight at Fan Fair 2001

(Keith, Randy, Michael, and Gwen) who became extensions of my family as I stayed at their home and worked with Jim and Jesse. I was another musical brother who stayed in the upstairs bedroom when I was in town.

I was one of the

© 2007 Joy McReynolds

Several of the Virginia Boys gather at the Pick Inn in Gallatin, Tennessee, in 2007. From left are, front row: Monroe Fields, Allen Shelton, Jesse McReynolds, Carol Johnson Bass, Rual Yarbrough; middle row: Dickie Mauldin, Jim Brock, Jr., Jim Brock Sr., Garrett McReynolds, Randall Franks; back row: Vic Jordan, Carl Jackson, Jim Buchanan (front), Donald Earl, Buddy Griffin, and Ashley Messenger.

Jim and Jesse — A Sound Unequaled

uncles to the grandchildren. Among them — Luke, Amanda Lynn, and Garrett became part of his Virginia Boys.

Jesse and I found energy in the efforts of innovation. We would spend hours exploring opportunities for a new promotion for Jim and Jesse or ways to better enhance their existing businesses.

Musically, there is no other Nashville star who invested so much into my future, sharing his talents and advice both on stage and in the studio. That is evident, if you review my discography.

As I stepped into the darkness backstage, it took a few minutes for my eyes to adjust.

© 2007 Randall Franks Media – Donna Tracy

Randall Franks (fourth from right) performs with Jesse and the other members of the Virginia Boys in Gallatin, Tennessee, in 2007.

When visiting the Grand Ole Opry, I often would stand near the back entrance of the stage in the darkness so I could get a view of all the folks milling around on stage. Stars like Faron Young, Pee Wee King, Jim Ed Brown, and Alison Krauss would pass by on their way to perform their number for the clamoring crowd, instruments in hand. Many would pause to say hello and shake hands.

As I stood there, one of those who passed and paused was Marty Stuart on his way to perform his "Hillbilly Rock." We talked briefly about some old pickin' buddies before he whisked away to do his thing for the crowd. Only a couple of years before, we sat around the campfire down in Florida at a bluegrass festival where he was performing as a guest with Jerry and Tammy Sullivan. I was there making an appearance with Doodle and the Golden River Grass.

As I stood there remembering, a hand appeared on my shoulder, and there stood Jesse McReynolds of Grand Ole Opry's Jim and Jesse. At that point in my career, I had been traveling on the road making appearances with their show. As Marty performed center stage while he was making his second run at the brass ring, Jesse said to me, "You know, if Marty can do that, you can." His popularity was soaring, for which all of us who knew him were proud.

Those words of encouragement from Jesse have always stuck in my ear.

While it was doubtful I would ever be considered rockabilly, which was where Marty was musically at the time, hearing those words from Jesse meant so much to me.

Jesse was saying that I could walk out center stage at

Randall Franks appears as a Jim and Jesse Show guest star at the Jekyll Island Bluegrass Festival in December 1994.

the Grand Ole Opry and be the star with my own major label recording deal.

Even as time has passed and we have said goodbye to Jim, Arreta, Darlene, and Keith; we have continued to work together behind the scenes to keep Jesse's latest project in the forefront.

As Jesse moved on with his life, he remarried, adding Joy to the family and thus yet another extended family member for me as well.

In recent years, I have been honored to join Jesse for birthday celebrations and reunions of the Virginia Boys at the Pick Inn, a wed-

Jim and Jesse — A Sound Unequaled

Randall Franks on the road with the Jim and Jesse Show in the 1990s. From left are Jim Buchanan, Jesse McReynolds, Jim McReynolds and Raymond McClain.

ding venue operated by Joy, on his farm near Gallatin.

Although I have not toured with him since the 1990s, he has graciously appeared on projects with me in recent years, and we still talk on the phone and make plans for his future musical endeavors.
I have told Jesse that he means a great deal to me, that there was a time in my life when he was as close as a father to me.

Unlike most of their generation's counterparts, they had worked steadily through all the ups and downs of the music industry.

One hope I had for Jim and Jesse was to see them get the recognition they deserve. I have seen some of the greats in all types of music walk up and do everything but bow at their feet saying that they had influenced their music. In the 1990s, the duo received the National Heritage Fellowship Award from the National Endowment for the Arts and a place in the International Bluegrass Music Association's Hall of Fame.

Not bad for a couple of boys from Carfax, a little Appalachian town in Virginia. Truly, they deserve induction into the Country

Encouragers

Music Hall of Fame. I thank Jim and Jesse for all they have done for me, and especially for all the enjoyment their music brings.

They came from the environment of Southern Virginia reflecting the hard work of the coal mines, farming or carving a living from the mountain region. Their grandfather Charles McReynolds was a renowned fiddler of the region recorded by RCA Victor. Jim and Jesse's parents were also accomplished musicians who played at square dances. From this rich musical background came the seeds that encouraged the brothers to begin a career that would take them around the world to become legends in their lifetimes.

Jim and Jesse began performing on a radio show on WNVA in 1947 in Norton, Virginia. This show marked the beginning of their association that only ended by Jim's passing in 2002.

The duo would eventually land at the Kentucky Barn Dance in Lexington, Kentucky, on WVLK by 1952. During this year, the brothers signed with Capitol Records.

It was not very long before the duo had to stop performing while Jesse served a tour of duty in Korea. After his return, Jim and Jesse joined the Tennessee Barn Dance on WNOX in Knoxville, Tennessee. They also made appearances on the Original WWVA Jamboree in Wheeling, West Virginia. South Georgia and North Florida became their home base region by 1955 as they gained sponsorships and were featured on countless radio and television shows on stations throughout the region. The biggest television partnership soon came with Martha White Foods. Over the next nine years they continued their steady rise to the Grand Ole Opry, performing on shows with many era stars such as Ernest Tubb, Roy Acuff, Bill Monroe, and Porter Wagoner.

Jim and Jesse's continuing work and success brought them to the Grand Ole Opry in 1964. The pivotal aspect of their musical relationship hinged between the brothers' blend of the vocals and the unique way their musicianship complemented their music. Jim's guitar and "clear polished tenor" set the duo apart from many other brother duets, while Jesse innovated mandolin playing. He created new approaches to playing, including cross picking and split stringing. He

106

always managed to include only the best musicians in their band.

Jim and Jesse recorded dozens of radio hits such as "Are You Missing Me", "Cotton Mill Man," "Diesel On My Tail," "Paradise," "Northwind," and "Ole Slew Foot." One of their biggest selling albums was entitled "Old Country Church," originally recorded for Epic Records. The album included many standards such as "Rock of Ages," "Lord, I Am Coming Home," "Swing Low, Sweet Chariot," and "Old Time Religion."

One of their most unusual albums is a collection of Rock 'n' Roll Chuck Berry songs — "Berry Pickin' Time in the Country." Through the album, they not only crossed musical barriers, bringing rock 'n' roll songs into mainstream country and bluegrass, but also at the height of the Civil Rights movement in 1965, they stepped out boldly as white country artists marketing an entire album of music from a black artist.

This album remains one of the most talked-about of their entire career, still drawing questions from interviewers as Jesse talks about his career five decades later. "Johnny B. Goode" remained a favorite request for the group throughout their performance career.

The group performed around the world in England, Europe, Africa, and the Far East. On one trip, they recorded Jim and Jesse "Live in Japan." Their appearances for foreign heads of state do not exceed the group's time performing at festivals and concerts across the United States and Canada. Jim and Jesse were true country music stars who appeared on all the great stages, television, and radio shows of their era. They even hosted their own syndicated country music television series called the Jim and Jesse Show.

Brian Bloom
Benji Wilhoite
Christian Slater
Randall Franks
Tammy Lauren
Randall Franks and Billy Vera

Randall Franks from the 1988 film *"Desperate for Love"*

The Wiseman's Path

To touch the purest essence of the voice of country music, as crisp as the cool air on a fall morning, look no further than the vibrant vocalist Mac Wiseman. He is one of the most prolific of the singers of the legendary generation that is credited with starting the genre of bluegrass. The distinctive style that he gives songs either makes them classics or endears them to an entirely new market of listeners. From his home in Nashville on February 7, 2006, at the age of eighty, he said that his recording work continued although his travel for appearances was reduced.

Mac Wiseman records at Home Place studio in Nashville in 1991.

"I'm still up to my keester in recording," he said. "My voice has held up well. I feel so fortunate."

In recent years, he has cut a gospel album with Charlie Daniels and another with John Carter Cash, completed the equivalent of three projects with Grand Ole Opry star Jesse McReynolds, and entered the studio to do a project with John Prine.

"I feel as good as I ever did," he said.

He had a seventy-one-year career that carried him from the Shenandoah Valley of Virginia through a parade of history making musical jobs with Molly O'Day, Curly Seckler, Flatt and Scruggs, and Bill Monroe and a solo career that brought him to the forefront of the country and pop music fields in the 1950s.

He left Flatt and Scruggs and joined Atlanta's WSB Barndance as its last shows were riding off into the sunset. Mac joined the cast in 1949, and shared the stage with entertainers such as Cotton Carrier, the Sunshine Boys, James and Martha Carson, and Bill Carlisle.

"We had the Barndance on the road at that time. It had been permanent out in East Point, a suburb of Atlanta, for quite a while, but then we started taking it around to different towns on Saturday and remoting it in through WSB," he said. "I had a daily radio program, worked shows out, and played WSB Barndance on Saturday. We had a darn good show."

For his contributions there, he was inducted into the Atlanta Country Music Hall of Fame; but the show closed only four months after Mac's arrival, precipitating his move to the Grand Ole Opry with Bill Monroe's Blue Grass Boys.

While he was there only a short time before embarking out on his own again, he looks on his Columbia recording session with Monroe as one of his greatest duets of his career.

"I came within a hair of not getting to record anything with him because he was on outs with Columbia because they signed the Stanley Brothers. He thought they were mimicking him and he didn't appreciate it," he said. "He owed Columbia another session, but Decca made him the offer but Columbia wouldn't release until he fulfilled the contract."

The thought of Mac's clear tones on Monroe's "Can't You Hear Me Calling" and "Traveling this Lonesome Road" still makes the hair on the back of my neck stand up.

Mac sees his association with Dot Records as the greatest opportunity that came in his career.

It was there that he cut his standards such as "Tis Sweet to Be Remembered," "Love Letters in the Sand," and "Jimmy Brown, the News Boy," among a long list of releases that included his hit "The Ballad of Davy Crockett."

He solidified for me the crossover potential of any song given the right singer. For traditional country, Mac was the right singer, but he carried his style to the field of pop music.

"I knew a long time back in the forties as I went from one radio

The Wiseman's Path

station to another like Atlanta and Knoxville and even the Opry," he said. "I knew that you had to be on record if you were going to make your mark at all, even though Dot was such a small label. There were only four or five major labels back then, and I was fortunate enough to get turned down by all of them.

"I had so much success with Dot Records and was able to call my own shots," he said. "As soon as I had a couple of releases then the majors came running, but I was loyal to Dot and it was good for me."

He found himself in 1957 and 1958 in the midst of the rock 'n' roll revolution.

"Rock 'n' roll was really upsetting our country music cart so to speak," he said. "Elvis and Jerry Lee (Lewis) and (Johnny) Cash were having tremendous success.

"I was on Old Dominion Barndance in Richmond, which was a 50,000 watt station and a show similar to the Opry," he said. "I could see the handwriting on the wall. It was going to take package shows. The days of the little act going out and playing schools and Grange Halls and theaters was fast on the way out."

Mac also had the unique ability to find a place for himself behind the scenes as well, serving as a record company executive, disc jockey, promoter, show producer, booking agent, and former Country Music Association officer.

His association with Dot would find him relocating to California to head the company's country and western division.
In the midst of his recording success he joined in package shows traveling across the U.S. and Canada where he was included among the leading country stars of the day. They included gigs with Ray Price, Ernest Tubb, the Maddox Brothers and Rose, and Ferlin Husky.

As the Folk Music Revival took hold, Mac marketed himself to college radio stations by sending each a couple of albums, moving himself among the elite sharing the folk music tradition with the baby boomers.

"I went through same repertoire I had on Dot, but a different group of people picked up on it, so I played the Newport Folk Festival several times, the New York Folk Festival, Philadelphia,

111

Encouragers

Mariposa, Toronto," he said. "I played the Mint three weeks in Vegas in 1963."

Growing from the success of the folk market was a new industry based on the acoustic music of the Appalachians.

"A lot of the folk music venues started recognizing the a la bluegrass music," he said. "Actually the term bluegrass did not come along until about that time. The reason for it being called that is the people in that field were looking for something to identify acoustical music.

"With Monroe being on the Opry and his group the Blue Grass Boys it seemed like the more natural thing to call it," he said, "Had his band been the Green Mountain Boys, we'd be calling it green mountain music."

The fledgling new genre of bluegrass had great limitations. Until 1965, there were no venues dedicated solely to its performance. Once an artist was identified as bluegrass, country radio stations began removing them from their Top 40 playlists and giving those spaces to artists who were considered more country — if that is even possible.

At the height of his career in country music, Mac Wiseman found himself locked out and placed alongside a group of noteworthy performers who included Bill Monroe, The Stanley Brothers, Jim and Jesse, Flatt and Scruggs, and others who were on the outside looking in on an industry that they themselves helped create.

"Bluegrass music was worst thing that ever happened to me," the International Bluegrass Music Association Hall of Fame member said. "I will hasten to explain that.

"Until that time, I got as much country play as Marty Robbins, Slim Whitman, Jim Reeves, and those guys and wasn't pigeon holed," Wiseman said. "When the concept of bluegrass came along and the radio stations would not play it at all, I was very limited and had to be very careful about what I recorded. There wasn't a market to take care of new songs."

As a classically trained artist who had only the limits of his imagination to carry him into whatever musical trail he desired to blaze, he was now placed by the music industry into a box that he and many others struggled to survive within.

"I made a terrible remark for bluegrass fans a while ago and hope they understand where I was going," he said. "Thank God for them because now we would not be able to work anywhere if it were not for the bluegrass festivals."

Mac was able to find a unique opportunity at the Wheeling Jamboree in West Virginia.

"The Feller (upstairs) that calls the shots opened another door, and I went up to run the Wheeling Jamboree from 1966-70," he said. "I also had a booking agency."

As the bluegrass industry was gaining stronger footing by 1969, Mac landed a contract with RCA and recorded several projects, including his hit "Johnny's Cash and Charley's Pride," and some of his favorite duet albums with Lester Flatt.

In my childhood of the seventies and eighties, I remember sitting barefooted in the summer heat looking up at him from the foot of bluegrass festival stages and anxiously waiting to hear this balladeer sing out with a power that could keep a windmill spinning for hours but tempered with a finesse that I have only heard in his voice.

On songs such as "Catfish John," "Me and Bobby McGee," and "I Wonder How the Old Folks Are At Home," he enriched my musical tastes. I could only wish to have the ease of performance that he shared as he connects with the audience.

While Mac settled into the bluegrass scene, he still sees himself as part of a much bigger musical picture. As an officer, he helped get the Country Music Association started in the late fifties, and he said he is disturbed by where the industry has gone.

"When we started out and formed the Country Music Association, it was direly needed. The rock 'n' roll Top 40 format was taking over," he said. "At that time, there were only one hundred and fifty stations in the U.S. playing any country music. I am not sure there were any full time. Now, there are over 2,500 stations.

"Some of these guys are selling more records on one release like these Garth Brooks and Alan Jackson than I probably sold in my career and making truckloads of money," he said. "I listen and like quite a bit of it.

"What disturbs me, its such a big business thing anymore there is not much heart or creativity in it," he said. "That is where we are dropping the ball right now. All the record companies now own the publishers, so naturally they are going to record songs they publish. Even the big stars, their careers are so short-lived, five or six years is about it. They just eat them up alive and burn them out and throw them away and get them another boy.

"They gross a lot of money, but there are a lot of deducts down the road — managers, agents, and publicists," he said. "By the time the bottom line gets along, it would knock your eyes out how little they have left.

"To start with, they act like Hollywood folk and buy racehorses and yachts and fancy cars and then have to work their tails off to pay for them."

I have enjoyed the pleasure of knowing Mac for nearly three decades. As my star began to rise in the music industry, I often shared the marquee with him on the road as we did package shows.

While I have learned a lot from Mac through the years, I think the greatest lesson was that when you are on stage, take command. He once told me whoever controls the microphone is in charge and that he was in charge each time he stepped out there.

One of the greatest opportunities in my life was getting to produce a vocal performance by him on the song "Christmas Time's A Comin'." I paired him with the tremendous talents of Jim and Jesse, and the harmonies of the threesome are still my favorite aspect of that recording.

He has recorded several CDs available on his own label featuring such classics as "Letter Edged in Black," "Just Because," and "Silver Haired Daddy," just to name a few.

"I got so many things I want to record that I do that nobody else does or knows. I have a list of over 200 songs I want to put out I know I never recorded," he said. "When I'm gone I'm afraid those songs will be lost because there is no documentation, published or put out in sheet music. I hope my voice holds out to document as many of those songs as I can."

When I spoke to him again on November 15, 2013, the 88-year-old was still excited about working on a new CD with Merle Haggard and recording alongside many new artists.

"It's very fulfilling to know you can contribute in a way to give people some happiness, some fulfillment, some joy," he said.

Mac is among the 2014 members of the Country Music Hall of Fame. His latest CD, "Songs From My Mother's Hand," includes songs his late mother wrote down from radio while he was a child.

And sent Timotheus, our brother, and minister of God, and our fellow labourer in the gospel of Christ, to establish you, and to comfort you concerning your faith:

1 Thessalonians 3:2

© 1988 Randall Franks Media – Ned D. Burris

Randall Franks — 1988

Earl Scruggs — The Banjo that Set the World on Fire

Earl Scruggs' (1924–2012) three-finger banjo style set the music world on its ear when he came to the stage of the Grand Ole Opry ® at the Ryman Auditorium alongside Bill Monroe in 1945.

As he and fellow Blue Grass Boy Lester Flatt left Monroe's band and set out to forge a career on their own, no one could have guessed they would become one of the best-known country acts in history. Lester Flatt, Earl Scruggs, and the Foggy Mountain Boys set the stage

© 2007 Regina Watkins

From left are Lorie Watkins, Todd Watkins (hidden), Lizzy Long, Randall Franks, Earl Scruggs and Randy Shelnut (hidden) on stage at the National Quartet Convention.

for what a traditional bluegrass band should be; and their music offered the template that others have only tried to emulate.

Thousands of banjo players around the world, including notables such as Steve Martin, credit their interest in the instrument to the innovations created by Scruggs.

Earl Scruggs, as he and Lester appeared on "The Beverly Hillbillies," inspired this young Appalachian musician's hopes and dreams of being on television someday.

As I set out on that path forged by them and the Dillards on "The Andy Griffith Show," I never imagined becoming a dramatic or comedic actor. I just thought I wanted to play my mountain music on television; but God had a different path in mind for me in order to reach that goal.

By the time I was big enough to attend bluegrass festivals, Earl and Lester many years earlier had split up in 1969. Earl had joined with his sons to create the Earl Scruggs Revue and was working major rock venues of that period. So my exposure to Earl in my early years was limited to his recordings and vintage TV reruns, until I met him and his wife Louise when Bill Monroe was mentoring me in 1984.

While I am not a banjo player, I still was always in awe of Earl, who graciously shared his time with me whenever I saw him or called him on the phone.

Years after becoming known as a network actor myself, I told Earl how much I appreciated the inspiration that he provided me as a child, helping me reach for the stars.

I was honored to join Earl on stage and perform with him at the National Quartet Convention. Among the tunes we performed was of course "The Ballad of Jed Clampett," and everyone will remember "The Foggy Mountain Breakdown." Amazingly, today as I write this, a tune entitled "Polka on the Banjo" from Flatt and Scruggs Martha White television shows is streaming through my head as I hear Curly Seckler's tenor ringing in my ears.

I thank God for giving certain people the spark that electrifies some piece of our existence and helps make life even greater for their presence. I think that is what Earl did. He was a humble, caring man who loved to play banjo and guitar, who cared for his family, his friends and who changed the music world and helped place the banjo in front of millions of people. Earl, I thank you for all you left behind for generations to come. I hope we play together again — I can just hear Earl's common lines heard on "The Beverly Hillbillies" echoing back — "Me too, (Randall). Me too …"

Dr. Ralph Stanley

If you are an aficionado of bluegrass, there is one thing for sure — when you say the name Stanley, one sound comes to mind — the mountain sounds of Carter and Ralph, The Stanley Brothers.

For those who feel a kinship to their Appalachian roots, there is hardly anyone who has a more distinctive mountain voice than that of the surviving Stanley brother — banjo stylist Dr. Ralph Stanley.

Ralph has carried that tradition for forty-nine years since the passing of his brother and carved out a niche for himself that has helped him ascend to the A-list of most elite musical performers in America. He has earned the National Medal of the Arts, Library of Congress's "Living Legend" medal, and the National Endowment for the Arts' National Heritage Fellowship award. Stanley

Randall Franks appears on stage for the Grand Ole Opry in 1985 with Ralph Stanley, Wilma Lee Cooper, and Bill Monroe.

received an honorary doctorate in 1976 from Lincoln Memorial University in Harrogate, Tennessee, and he has been known as "Dr. Ralph" ever since. Yale University gave him a second honorary doctor of music degree in 2014.

I have had the pleasure to be a fan of his throughout my life. I met Ralph more than twenty-five years ago, and I've had the honor to play with him on stage on numerous occasions for the Grand Ole Opry when Bill Monroe would feature an array of bluegrass stars in a jam

Encouragers

session together on stage. I have appeared at his annual Memorial Bluegrass Festival near McClure, Virginia, and shared the bill with him at numerous festivals around the country.

One of the greatest days of my life was when he walked into a Nashville studio where I actually got to produce this master at work.

I had the pleasure to sit down with now Grand Ole Opry star Ralph Stanley and interview him in 2007 and gather his unique perspective on a number of experiences:

Me: Like so many of your contemporaries, you hit the road for decades, keeping a band and a bus going. When you reached your seventies, you hit superstar status, being reborn to the MTV generation somewhat like Tony Bennett. Did you ever anticipate attaining some of the opportunities you have in the last decade?

Ralph: No, not really. When that (film) "O Brother, Where Art Thou?" came along and I got to sing the song ("Oh, Death") on the soundtrack. (This 2000 Coen Brothers comedy set in the rural 1930s south starred George Clooney.), that really put the icing on the cake for me. I had recorded some CDs with about all the traditional country artists. (Some among those were Josh Turner, George Jones, Patty Loveless, Vince Gill, Marty Stuart, Alison Krauss, and Dolly Parton.) That wasn't hurting me any. It helped me a lot you know. I give that soundtrack of "O Brother, Where Art Thou?" the most credit for it.

Me: Mr. Stanley, in recent years you were honored with an induction in the Grand Ole Opry, and the Ralph Stanley Museum and Traditional Mountain Music Center opened in Clintwood, Virginia, highlighting your contributions. You've received countless awards, including Grammys. Is there one award that is what it is all for?

Ralph: My highlight is when I won the (2002) Grammy for the Best Country Vocalist of the Year. (He was included in a field with Johnny Cash, Willie Nelson, Lyle Lovett, Tim McGraw, and Ryan Adams.) As far as I know, I don't know of any singer like me old time bluegrass to be nominated and win a country category. I guess that was about my highlight. I enjoyed getting on the Grand Ole Opry. Any entertainer looks forward to that.

Me: Is there one song you performed in your career that is your

Dr. Ralph Stanley

favorite?

Ralph: That's a hard question. I've been asked that before. That "Man of Constant Sorrow" would be hard to turn down. Of course, I didn't sing it on the soundtrack of "O Brother," but I recorded way back in 1948 and kept it alive all through the years. That might be the song.

Me: Do you think the music industry has gotten to the point that so much of the music sounds alike?

Ralph: There is so much music that you don't know who is singing it unless you are looking at them. When you hear my music, you know who it is without looking at me.

Me: With music historians in mind, what would you say is your greatest contribution?

Ralph: Everybody tells me, and I guess it's right, there has never been a voice just like mine. It goes a way back. When I first started, people said, I sounded like it was one hundred years old. It's just an old time voice that I am proud that God gave me. I don't care where you go. I've never heard another voice like it. It's my voice much more than my music. For more information, visit drralphstanleymusic.com.

© 1991 Randall Franks Media – Ben Hall

Randall Franks produces Ralph Stanley at
Home Place studio in Nashville in 1991.

The Marksmen Quartet — 1987
From left (front) are Randall Franks, Mark Wheeler, Keith Chambers, (back)Rob Gillentine, Earle Wheeler, and Darrin Chambers.

Chubby Wise

As I look back on the fiddlers who most impacted my life, one of those would be Bluegrass Music Hall of Fame member Chubby Wise (1915–1996). I knew his music from the beginning of picking up the instrument, although there has even been a book written saying his contribution to the classic fiddle song "Orange Blossom Special" was not plausible and his story did not match with its creation by Ervin Rouse and the Rouse Brothers.

For decades, he maintained he did create it, and personally, I don't think he had any reason to claim involvement falsely, and since to my knowledge, he never received a penny from the song, he gained only prestige by saying it. He already had that.

He told me his story of what occurred and if in his heart, he felt he contributed to it, I am not going to dispute his word even if others do. In a way, it is part of the mystique of the history of our country music genre.

Randall Franks and Chubby Wise harmonize in a Jacksonville, Florida, studio in 1991.

Chubby was one of the original five members of Bill Monroe's Blue Grass Boys that hit the notes that created the essential classic bluegrass sound at the Grand Ole Opry in 1946 with Lester Flatt, Earl Scruggs, and Howard Watts.

He performed with Clyde Moody, co-writing his hit "The Shenandoah Waltz," performed and recorded with Flatt and Scruggs and the Foggy Mountain Boys, Mac Wiseman, Hank Williams, Sr., and Elton Britt.

His longest run was as part of Hank Snow's Rainbow Ranch Boys

Encouragers

where he spent nearly sixteen years on the Grand Ole Opry followed by another fourteen years touring from Texas before moving back to Lake City, Florida, in 1984.

By the time I came to know Chubby and his wife Rossie while they were in Florida, he was making solo appearances at bluegrass festivals with the backing of regional and national acts hired by the promoter to support the legend as he came onto the stage looking like Santa Claus playing the fiddle.

His easy, down-home appeal with the audience endeared him in a way that the audience was easily mesmerized as he played a famous list of tunes that he pop-ularized.

© 1991 Ronald Stuckey – Randall Franks Media

Randall Franks and Chubby Wise perform on stage at the Sleepy Hollow Bluegrass Festival on January 19, 1991 in Brooksville, Florida.

I always loved to see him perform with the Boys from Indiana because they narrated his appearance and sup-ported him vocally, bringing the Chubby Wise discography to life on stage.

Chubby became my friend and mentor, not only teaching me but also welcoming me on stage again and again to play twin fiddle with him in front of audiences that loved him. By doing so, he essentially shared his audience with me and in many ways set the stage for me to carry on the traditions and rapport he established with them.

In many ways, I have tried to do that. The milestones he created cannot be recreated, but I am honored to invoke his memory and share my memories of him as I travel and play.

I am also honored as I watch after his musical publishing legacy as well.

The King of Bluegrass

One of the most flamboyant individuals I ever had the opportunity to work with is bluegrass and country music icon Jimmy Martin (1927–2005).

His ability to steal the show is legendary. His heartfelt voice captured the attention and the emotions of the audience as he brightened their eyes with colorful costumes and his winning smile.

Randall Franks and Jimmy Martin pause between recordings in Nashville in 1991.

It is difficult to describe my own feelings about this Bluegrass Hall of Fame member. I sent him a letter detailing my appreciation to him for what he had done for me in my life as he neared the end of his journey to which he quickly responded.

I enjoyed Jimmy's energy and his will to endure, no matter what obstacles came in front of him. I learned a great deal from him, and his absence from the bluegrass family is a void that can never be filled.

I had the pleasure of producing Jimmy in the Home Place studio in Nashville, Tennessee, in 1991.

For my entire life, I had heard some tall tales about Jimmy's antics — his passion for coon and squirrel hunting and his tendency to enjoy late night jam sessions.

When the Nitty Gritty Dirt Band did its original "Will The Circle Be Unbroken" albums in 1972, it was Jimmy who came into a studio with legends like Mother Maybelle, Roy Acuff, and Doc Watson and stole the gold record-earning project with his performances of the

Encouragers

"Sunny Side of the Mountain," and the "Grand Ole Opry Song" among others.

Jimmy was let go from a factory job in 1949 and he decided to come to Nashville. With sheer will, he worked his way backstage at the Grand Ole Opry, convinced Bill Monroe to audition him, and won a job as his guitar player and lead singer.

The combination of these two voices created what many classify as the high lonesome sound of bluegrass. Martin remained for roughly five years creating classics such as "The Little Girl and the Dreadful Snake" and "Uncle Pen." He and the Osborne Brothers teamed up for about a year creating songs such as "20/20 vision" before Jimmy went out on his own.

© 1991 Randall Franks Media – Donna Tracy

From left, Ralph Stanley, Jimmy Martin, and Randall Franks visit backstage at the CMA Fan Fair Bluegrass Show in 1991.

With his Sunny Mountain Boys, he regularly created hit songs among the hundreds of songs he recorded. These made him a constant presence in both country and bluegrass radio. He was with Decca Records for almost two decades until the mid-70s and then he signed with Starday/Gusto.

Among my favorites are hits "Widow Maker" and "Sunny Side of the Mountain."

While I never worked with him on stage, as we sat in his living room, we did discuss going out on the road together. Me performing

The King of Bluegrass

with his Sunny Mountain Boys — what an honor that would have been to perform with a band that fostered talent like J.D. Crowe and Doyle Lawson. Unfortunately, it never worked out.

I cherish the many times we visited. One of my favorite records he did was a joint project with Ralph Stanley entitled "Our First Time Together." To me it was the epitome of the bluegrass sound, that also joined two legends.

One of my favorite childhood memories is seeing Jimmy and his Sunny Mountain Boys at bluegrass festivals such as Lavonia. I learned a great deal from his stage presence and use many of the techniques I saw him employ.

I remember at some point he did a Christmas album called "To Mother at Christmas." He was promoting it from the stage in the middle of summer. You know what? He sold them. His charisma is amazing.

He became the focus of the film entitled "King of Bluegrass." The documentary follows Jimmy's lifelong quest to reach his childhood dream of becoming a regular cast member of the Grand Ole Opry — a goal never attained but richly deserved.

But the God of all grace, who hath called us unto his eternal glory by Christ Jesus, after that ye have suffered a while, make you perfect, stablish, strengthen, settle you.

1 Peter 5:10

Randall Franks — 1988

Raymond Fairchild — Smoky Mountain Banjo King

When I began touring in the bluegrass circuit, one of the most unique characters that added color to the palette of musical masters that graced the stages of the festivals was Raymond Fairchild.

A Cherokee hailing from Cherokee, North Carolina, he was heralded as the fastest banjo player in history.

His approach to the instrument was all his own, though he looked to Earl Scruggs and Don Reno as his professional inspirations. His early influences came from his maternal aunt Martha Ballew who played the banjo left-handed.

Fairchild

"I went between Scruggs and Reno and came up with what people now call the Fairchild style. Jimmy Martin and Bill Monroe even said that there were three styles of banjo playing — Scruggs, Reno and Fairchild," Raymond said in a 2014 interview.

When I first came to know Raymond, his stoic, no nonsense demeanor would have made him a perfect tough heavy in any movie. As a youth, I found him intimidating, especially knowing he didn't take anything off anyone.

If I had not come to know him personally, I might have kept that opinion, but during my time fiddling for Doodle and the Golden River Grass, his friendship with Doodle Thrower allowed me the opportunity to come to know him and include him among my friends.

By that time, he had perfected his stage show with the support of Josh and Wayne Crowe — The Crowe Brothers. Josh did the emcee work, and the brothers sang duets while supporting Raymond in his smokin'-hot pickin'. Eventually, Raymond's son Zane added to the unit, playing guitar.

Raymond began sharing his talents professionally in the late 1950s at Ted Sutton's Hillbilly Campground in Maggie Valley, North Carolina, performing for tourists.

"We played for tips there at Sutton's for many years," he said.

Raymond recalled that Dalton musician Curly Bigham brought him from Maggie Valley to Dalton and introduced him to the late

Encouragers

radio host and businessman Otis Head where Fairchild started doing shows for him at his Plainview Superette.

"He started picking the banjo at the supermarket," Head said.

Otis recalled seeing Raymond in Maggie Valley and felt having him at his store could only enhance his business.

"He got to drawing such a crowd," he said. "I had to stop cause it was hurting my business. I could not do business with all the people there. They did not come to trade, they came to watch him pick."

At the same time, Otis was making contact with friends in Nashville, telling them about Raymond. Before long, Otis had Raymond in Nashville recording his first album "America's Most Authentic Folk Banjo" for the Sims label released in the early 1960s.

Randall Franks on stage with Raymond Fairchild and his band in 2003.

"I sold a lot of those on the roadside stand shows at Sutton's," Raymond said.

That first album began a long professional career that opened doors in Nashville and prepared the stage for Raymond to set the world of traditional music on fire. He won five consecutive Master of the Banjo championships and took the stage of the Grand Ole Opry by storm in 1978. He credits Nashville doctor Nat Winston for initially getting him on the Opry. In his long discography, he includes two gold records for Rural Rhythm among a long list he recorded for the

Raymond Fairchild — Smoky Mountain Banjo King

company.

Eventually, after many years together, he and the Crowe Brothers parted ways and Raymond rebuilt his stage presentation and added other musicians. Once nearly com-

Randall Franks appears in Maggie Valley with Raymond Fairchild in 2014.

© 2014 Randall Franks Media

pletely silent on stage except for his banjo, Raymond took over the emcee work. Through the years, many talented musicians have graced the stage with Raymond but ultimately what the folks came to hear is Raymond play the banjo.

I've always enjoyed opportunities to share time with Raymond on stage and off. He has welcomed me on his show on several occasions, and we have also staged package shows featuring us both. Selections from these joint appearances have become very popular for us on YouTube, featuring some of his talented Maggie Valley Boys including Bruce Moody, Cody Shuler, and Eddie Lovelace. He has become one of my long-time friends and encouragers in bluegrass. We have spent many in-depth conversations where he has shared lessons learned from the greats we both admired.

Even though his banjo has taken him many miles, Raymond is quick to point to his times at Sutton's as some of his fondest memories of doing something he loved, makin' more money than he ever made before while being at home in Maggie Valley.

He now hosts his own show nightly from May through October at the Maggie Valley Opry House where folks can see his countless awards, accolades and accomplishments. Learn more by visiting http://www.raymondfairchild.com.

© 1986 The Golden River Grass

Doodle and the Golden River Grass — 1986
From left are Randall Franks, Wesley Clackum, Doodle
Thrower, Gene Daniell, and James Watson.

Charlie Cline

One of RCA's original Lonesome Pine Fiddlers — Bluegrass Hall of Fame member Charles "Charlie" Cline (1931-2004) — came from a musical family that also brought us Ralph Stanley's long-time fiddle sidekick, Curly Ray Cline. Charlie was one of the greatest who ever made the instrument sing.

I had the pleasure of being able to call Charlie my friend for many years. He remains ever present in my memory, as he would take on one of the many cartoon-type character vocal routines he might pull. After I became a cop on television, he often would put on a James Cagney type voice, joking with me, "You'll never get me coppeeeer."

We shared the honor of both being alumni of Bill Monroe's Blue Grass Boys; but even more than that, he and I traveled the highways and byways as I made special appearances with David Davis and the Warrior River Boys.

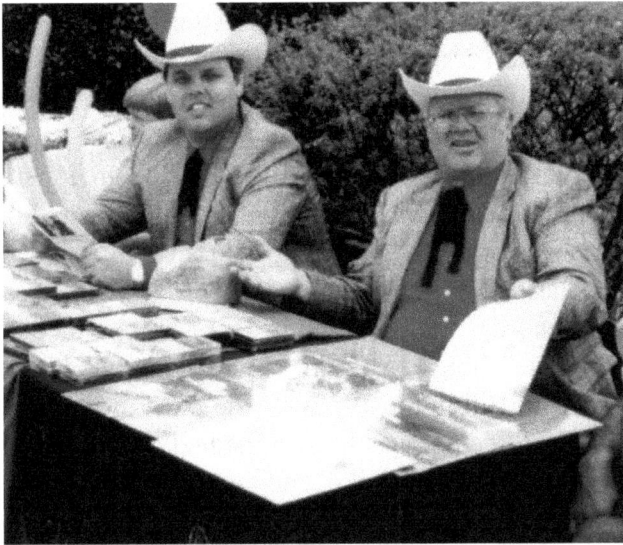

Charlie Cline (right) works his record table at an appearance with the Warrior River Boys in 1990 in Georgia beside banjo picker Larry Wallace.

As a legend in the business, Charlie provided an air of unique connection to the history that came before in that he was responsible for many of the musical licks and vocal performances that were classics among the repertoire of Monroe, Jimmy Martin, and the Lonesome Pine Fiddlers.

"The thing I think about Charlie is he was not one to look for a

133

Encouragers

pat on the back for his past in music," said David Davis. "He appreciates someone for having knowledge on what he accomplished, but the main thing that drove him was walking in God's light and living a life pleasing to the Lord and trying to share that with the people he was around. That was the thing I think was great about Charlie Cline."

Davis said that Charlie graciously came to work with his group in 1987, leaving Jimmy Martin's bus and crawling into a van with four twenty-something musicians.

"He never complained, and we were traveling a tremendous amount," he said. "When I look back in those times there was a good bit of age difference between us. After he left here in 1991, I often found myself responding with a stock quote that Charlie would say. I find myself understanding more of what he said then about music or life than I did at the time."

Davis said that Charlie was one of the great performers that music stars of that era needed because he could do anything — sing, play all the instruments and do comedy routines.

"Charlie played banjo on Jimmy Martin's first recordings with King Records, after Jimmy left Bill Monroe, on classics like 'She's Just a Cute Thing,'" he said. "I understand he was on thirty to forty songs with Bill in the 1950s — the most defining period of Bill's music; and if truth was known, he had a big part in creating fiddle classics such as 'Roanoke' and 'Wheel Hoss.'"

Davis also said Charlie's distinctive harmonies rounded out many of Monroe's classic trios such as on "Voice from on High" and "On and On."

"I think he was first to record lead guitar with the Stanley Brothers on Mercury Records in the early fifties and one of the first to do it with Monroe," he said. "He even played mandolin for Monroe through a stretch when Bill broke his collarbone.

"To me, he was one of the best of his time," he said. "He knew how to entertain, and he learned in the old way."

Charlie was a dedicated family man, musician, and a devoted evangelist as well.

Time with him was always an adventure. He was in constant

Charlie Cline

Randall Franks backed by Charlie Cline's band
at Toro Hills Bluegrass Festival in Louisiana in 1995.

motion, always coming up with some little joke or prank to pull or gain a laugh from road-weary troubadours in the tight confines of a van or even some antics to bring the crowd to its knees while on stage.

He was always entertaining even if it was just for a waitress in a truckstop or someone standing across the record table looking at his wide variety of merchandise.

I learned a lot about merchandising from Charlie; he always had the ability to sell just about anything from his record table.

Throughout his career, when not working with other acts, he would revive the Lonesome Pine Fiddlers to tour, often with his wife, Lee, at his side. One of my last appearances with the great Cline was at Toro Hills in Louisiana when I asked the promoter to hire his band to back me on my shows at a new bluegrass festival there.

It was a great honor to once again walk on the stage with him, and he was in rare form.

Any instrument in his hands seemed just as at home as the fiddle, but the fiddle will always be synonymous with the name Charlie Cline. As Chi Chi Rodriguez electrified the game of golf with his energy and unusual antics, if there was ever a Chi Chi Rodriguez of fiddling, Charlie was it.

© 1989 Randall Franks Media

Randall Franks — 1989

Pickin' and Grinnin' Friends
Gospel Music

A Visit with Bill Gaither

(On February 11, 2003, I had the opportunity to sit down with one of my music heroes, the legendary Bill Gaither.)

As you flip through the cable channels these days at any given hour on any given day, there is a tremendous chance you will find a scene with a group of loving and caring people gathered in a circle around a piano making a joyful noise unto the Lord.

Whether you are a believer or not, the warm sense of family that is conveyed in that moment of channel surfing can easily welcome a viewer to pull up a chair and sing along. That is what millions upon millions have done as Bill and Gloria Gaither have brought their Homecoming Friends to the screen in television specials, videos, and music albums of all forms.

What started purely as an accident is now one of the music industry's biggest phenomena. Two decades ago, Bill Gaither gathered together some of his gospel music heroes to join the Gaither Vocal Band on one song, "Where Would I Go But to the Lord?"

Gaither said it all started when, "Larry Gatlin said, 'Eva Mae, play something.'"

Eva Mae is Eva Mae LeFevre (1917–2009) of the LeFevres.

Eva Mae

"She started playing. They started singing," he said. "I did not know that there was a camera watching. I did not even know the mic was on. We were just playing and singing for the joy of playing and singing."

When he discovered the spontaneous event had been taped, Gaither asked for the footage, took it home, and edited it for the first "Homecoming" video.

From this one unplanned event came a series of videos that continue to comfort and touch millions around the world. More than ten million copies of the videos in the series have been sold.

Such an accomplishment is not bad for a boy raised in the cornfields of Indiana, a boy who started his career as an English teacher.

Gaither compares his success to "a turtle sitting on the fence post; the turtle did not get there by himself." Through his work he continues to pay homage to his gospel music heroes, like the Statesmen, the LeFevres, the Blackwood Brothers, the Speers, and so many more.

Encouragers

When the Bill Gaither Trio started out, there was no place for them to fit in gospel music; essentially they were on the outside looking in at the Southern gospel quartet music that he loved.

Bill Gaither and Randall Franks

"My brother (Danny) and my wife were not strong enough to compete in that marketplace," he said. "Those guys had big voices and they had big endings and would tear the house up. Gloria could not sing a loud note if she had too. So we just had to back off and write some songs that we could sing."

With the support of J.D. Sumner, the trio made its first appearance in the sixties at the National Quartet Convention in Memphis. The group did not receive a tremendous reception.

"I never saw the backs of so many people in my life," he said. "I think half the crowd got up and went to the bathroom while we were singing because we were just soft, easy, laid-back kind of singers, and they were used to hard-sell, driving, and getting on your mule and getting that thing done."

Once Bill and Gloria's songs started to catch on, the Gaithers almost single-handedly created the Inspirational radio format, filling the airwaves with their self-penned songs, "Because He Lives," "The King Is Coming," "He Touched Me," "Something Beautiful," and "There Is Something About That Name." For their writing, Bill and Gloria Gaither were named American Society of Composers, Authors and Publishers' Christian Songwriters of the Century based on the airplay of their songs.

140

A Visit with Bill Gaither

Over the last two decades, Bill and Gloria Gaither's Homecoming Friends videos have been a unifying force in gospel music and around the world. In times of trial, people often turn to God for comfort, and the music is often what helps deliver that message.

"When you sing a song like 'Hold To God's Unchanging Hand,' which is a hundred years old," he said, "you know the writer knew about an eternal truth — that there would be hard times."

"My lands! The times we have lived in since 9/11 in our country have been the most scary times we have had probably for a long time," he said.

Gaither said songs with staying power "stick on the wall." In Bill and Gloria Gaither's endless stream of creative and unique songs, many stick on the wall.

"When we wrote 'Because He Lives,' I thought it was good, but I did not know it was going to have quite the impact that it has had again and again," he said. "It seems to have (an impact) at life-and-death moments."

Gaither said people write to him often and share how that song has brought them through the torment of losing a child.

He recently received a letter that shared the effect that "Because He Lives" had on former President Richard Nixon following his resignation.

A professor named Wendell Campbell sent President Nixon an album of "Alleluia" and later received a call from the president. He thanked him for the gift that moved him deeply and encouraged him.

"I've played that (selection) so many times that I've about worn out that song on the album," Nixon said to Campbell.

At this point in his career, even Gaither has his critics that he says he can learn from, but many believe he is currently the biggest force in gospel music.

Gaither said he is just doing something that he believes in "very, very much."

"The critics would say that (what we do) is not Southern gospel as (they) define it," he said. "By their definition it is pretty narrow. In my case it is great soloists. It is a little bit of black soul. It is a little bit of bluegrass, a little bit of fiddles. I have been able to combine a lot of different kinds of tastes, which has proven to me there is a broader audience. I did not expand my walls for this reason; I expanded simply because of my tastes. I love what I do. I love to listen to what I do."

The Gaither Vocal Band performs in Chattanooga in November 2007.

© 2007 Randall Franks Media – Randall Franks

Gaither said "music is the most divisive element in our culture today."

"The person who said that music is a universal language lied. That is a lie," he said. "If you do not think it is divisive, take a vacation with your kids the next time in a stationwagon or whatever they travel in today and try to find a radio station that the whole family can agree on. You can't. It all is divided on the basis of musical preference."

"When I was a kid in the fifties, there was a pop song of the week that everybody could sing," he said. "It was on the Top 10 Lucky Strike Countdown on television. That week everybody would be singing 'How Much Is That Doggie In the Window' or whatever the dumb song was, and every now and then it was a beautiful love song."

"We had these moments to remember," he said. "You could not get a quorum today in our culture to say what the top song of the day is — nobody knows.

"The things I have done with the videos the last ten years is I have gone back to songs that build instant community the minute you start singing, songs like "Beulah Land," he said. "Everybody would join in and sing it. The people in that circle will.

"We taught a college Sunday school class a couple of years ago at our church at Anderson, (Indiana)" he said. "We could not find a common group of songs when we were at a campfire."

In one of his video projects, Gaither looked toward "Heaven" and "Going Home." These videos are a wonderful combination of music and inspirational words that help to connect the viewer to what Heaven and the journey there will be.

"It is more than just about Heaven; it is about facing life with an eternal perspective," he said.

Gaither recalled the words of Thornton Wilder's stage manager in "Our Town" — "We all know down deep there is something eternal. It ain't a house and it ain't property and it ain't farmland. It ain't even a star. We all know surely there is something that is going to live on beyond this. Because life does not make sense."

"The problem with all of us when we start getting things is we want more things," he said. "And we think this is going to go on and on forever.

"I suppose the poets, the preachers, singers, and the actors have to remind us from time to time that this ain't it. This is just the rehearsal," he said. "Does that mean we need to be escapists and escape reality? No."

"('Heaven') is the first video we have done where the content — the talking or verbiage — is more important than the songs because we have got a lot of comments from thinkers, pastors and leaders," he said.

The video's inspiring words come from a wide variety of thinkers from Mark Twain to Billy Graham.

"Up front, it sounds like it could be a sad, depressing thing, but it really is not," he said. "It is realistic. It ends up with 'When the Saints Go Marching In' 'cause black churches have done it better than we have done it for years; because it is a celebration."

Find out more about Bill Gaither by visiting www.gaithernet.com.

Randall Franks — 1989

Archie Watkins

If there is a voice that has made a mark on the sound of Southern gospel music, it is that of Archie Watkins.

The Southern Gospel Music Hall of Fame member was featured vocalist on more chart

Archie Watkins (right) joins Share America president Randall Franks and secretary James Pelt (left) for the Pearl and Floyd Franks Scholarship presentation to Ryan Stinson (second from right) in 2012.

songs than any other singer in gospel music history.

Singing News subscribers previously voted him Favorite Male Singer three times and Favorite Tenor four times.

Throughout my life, each time I've heard him sing, the hair on the back of my neck stands up. He just has a voice that is distinctive above all others in our industry.

His song "Two Shoes" has always brought a tear to my eyes, and number ones like "I'll Not Turn My Back on Him Now" and "Touring the City" have always been uplifting to me.

Archie is a good man who loves God, and he has given so much of his life to uplift the lives of others through music. He enjoys time with his family, hunting and, of course, sharing His love of Jesus through song.

He is no stranger to travel with more than forty-five years under his belt singing tenor with the Inspirations of Bryson City, North Carolina. He decided to resign from that group in 2009 and begin a new phase of his life singing solo dates. Within a couple of years he

Encouragers

added performances with old friends Troy Burns, Eddie Deitz, Marlin Shubert, and the old bear hunter the late Jack Laws. They became known as Archie Watkins and the Smokey Mountain Reunion.

"It's been overwhelming. I can't believe what has happened," he said.

"When I started working on the first solo project, the Lord gave us some good songs," he said. "We put up a website, and before I could turn around I had thirty dates booked."

Those thirty turned into one hundred twenty as the first year progressed.

"It's nothing I am doing," he said. "It is in the hands of the Lord. All that matters is I am doing it for the right purpose and the spirit of the Lord is in it."

© 2013 Share America Foundation

Archie Watkins and Randall Franks share a duet in 2013.

The solo career is taking he and his wife Cindy around the Southeast. He likes to tie hunting in whenever he can.

"A lot of what I do is schedule singing and hunting together," he said. "We love RVing for twenty years. We've always liked to camp. We have an RV, and going to sing is like going on an RV trip."

He said though he has been on the road fifty years it's like seeing it all new again.

"For forty-five years we rode, we'd ride to where we were going to be," he said. "We never did see so much of the open road. We run the two lane roads and see the country. You do not have to go far to have a good vacation ... Everything is so beautiful."

For more information, visit www.archiewatkins.com.

Stand By the River — Dottie Rambo

{I had the pleasure August, 28, 2003, to sit down with one of my favorite people, Grammy winner Dottie Rambo (1934–2008).}

When you think about all the great musical sounds and words that have influenced our society over the last century, one cannot help but consider songs such as "He Looked Beyond My Faults and Saw My Needs," "We Shall Behold Him," "Too Much to Gain to Lose," and "I've Never Been This Homesick Before." When I first heard these songs, I felt closer to God and heaven than I ever had before.

Dottie Rambo gives a TV interview at Ringgold United Methodist Church in April 2007.

The craft of songwriting is one that takes years to perfect; however, one can never reach total perfection. I personally believe that the songs that truly touch people's hearts are not just crafted by the writer but are freely given to them by God through the Holy Spirit touching their souls.

One night I had the pleasure of seeing the instrument through which God gave us these wonderful songs in a performance on the Trinity Broadcasting Network (TBN) in 2003. God had restored Dottie Rambo's once frail body to a strength I had not seen in her in some time.

"The energy, the anointing, my posture was so much better," she

Encouragers

said. "I could stand and hit those songs. It is remarkable how far I have come."

After facing tremendous illness, Dottie Rambo returned to the forefront of the music scene with her CD, "Stand by the River," from Spring Hill Music Group after an eighteen-year hiatus from recording.

Years ago, a back surgery gone wrong sidelined her monumental career by paralyzing her on one side.

"I had been so long in bed when my spine was mutilated," she said. "When you do that, your vocal chord is the main muscle that will go first. I wanted to start singing again. I went to a music teacher to help me with the vocal chord muscle. She really helped me.

"I did not ever think I would be able to come back," she said. "I never dreamed I could make a CD and have that strong voice back again. I should have. The Lord knows when He is ready for you to get back out there with the people."

God spoke to her through the Holy Spirit in a dream encouraging her to sing again.

"In my dream I was sitting in this dark cave, and it was pouring rain outside," she said. "I was an eagle, and my wing had been broken. The feathers were falling off. I had splints on both wings. I was trembling. I was so weak. In that vision, that voice said to me 'Take your splints off your wings, jump out on this ledge, get out in the world, and spread those wings. They are healed. Now you go and fly.' That is when I started to get back into writing and music."
In 2002, with God's help she overcame three comas to come back and give the world that project.

That CD included some of her favorite songs from the past combined with brand-new compositions. The title cut, "Stand By The River," a duet with Dolly Parton, was nominated in three award categories, including the 2003 Song Of The Year by the Christian Country Music Association.

Dottie said the hit song was not even supposed to be on the tape forwarded to Dolly for consideration; only a piece of it was there. "Dolly and I are like sisters," she said. "She called and said if we are going to record, I want the last song on the tape and, it was 'Stand By

Stand By the River — Dottie Rambo

the River.' It did so well.

"I wrote a fact and fiction song ("West Kentucky Coalmines") for the CD," she said. "I said to my producer Michael Sykes you may not agree this song should be on the CD."

"I had a brother crushed in the mines," she said. "He lost all the muscle from the elbow to the shoulder, but he is a fighter like me. He started therapy up until that boy got that muscle back."

The song tells the story of forty trapped miners in Union County, Kentucky.

"We are getting a lot of good feedback on that song, and they are now wanting to push it into the country field," she said.

My favorite song on the CD, "I'm Going to Leave Here Shouting," is an upbeat hand-clapper that recounts the title from something her grandfather said as he waited to meet God. Songwriter of the century Dottie Rambo is someone who certainly goes to the rock for strength, direction, and inspiration. She was the focus of the More than the Music

© 2007 Randall Franks Media

Dottie Rambo
and Randall Franks

Encouragers

video, DVD, and CD tribute entitled "We Shall Behold Him." The project features some of gospel, bluegrass, and country's greatest stars including host Barbara Mandrell, Larry Gatlin, Dolly Parton, Crystal Gayle, Vestal Goodman, the Isaacs, and many more honoring Rambo.

Dottie said the night she performed on this tribute, she unknowingly suffered from a collapsed lung and double pneumonia. The next morning she entered the hospital, went into a coma, and doctors placed her on life support.

"It was everything I could do to even hit a note on pitch," she said.

When watching the tribute and her performance, it is amazing what Dottie was able to do considering her condition. Her performance was certainly inspiring that evening at the Ryman Auditorium in Nashville, Tennessee.

From the first song she wrote at age eight while sitting on a brook bank near her Morganfield, Kentucky, home, Rambo said she felt something special.

"I loved to be alone, so I would go down there and sit with my feet in the water, and one day I felt this incredible, wonderful feeling like that which came over me when Grandpa would pray," she said.

She ran home to her mother who was baking pies in the kitchen to share the new song. Her mother just kept on working and she asked Dottie, "Baby, did you write that from a songbook somewhere?"

"No, ma'am," she said.

"She hugged me, cried, and said 'Little Dottie, you are going to pay a great price for this gift,'" she said. "I had no idea what she was talking about. She was abused by my father in many ways. I was mentally abused by my father."

Dottie began her singing career performing country music. "(At age 11) I had been with a country-western band on the radio on Saturdays," she said. "I was doing some Chet Atkins-style guitar playing. It was a good group. I still like country and western."

Dottie's childhood choice to do gospel music changed her life.

"When I was converted at almost twelve (years old), I went down to hear a man I heard on the radio," she said. "He started preaching,

Stand By the River — Dottie Rambo

Dottie Rambo on stage with
Randall Franks and Garrett Arb

and I got nervous. It was the first time I felt conviction. I realized I was shaking the pew. It was the first time I ever felt someone preaching the word to me. When he came back to me, he said 'Little Dottie, you need Jesus.' I almost pushed him out of the way, and said, 'I know it, so I can get down there (and pray).'

"I cannot tell you the peace that came over me," she said. "I told my mother and my dad what I done. Dad had a fit. I traveled (singing) with my daddy. He gave me an option when I was converted of either singing country or gospel. If I sang gospel, I was not welcome there. I left (home) at twelve years old, and I never looked back."

From that point, she went forth to create more than 2,500 songs that greats in every field of music have recorded.

Whitney Houston performed her Dove Award-winning "I Go to the Rock" in the film "The Preacher's Wife."

Sandy Patti's performance of "We Shall Behold Him" garnered

numerous awards for both her and Dottie.

Dottie said she and Elvis were close friends. When Elvis passed away in 1977, he had completed one song — "If That Isn't Love" — of a Dottie Rambo tribute album he was doing.

"I was with him a lot. He asked me if I would open up his show (in Las Vegas)," she said. "I wanted to so badly. But in my heart of hearts, I did not want to get that far away. You can get caught up and lose your own ability to write your own music."

Many others have recorded her songs, including Dolly Parton, Barbara Mandrell, Dottie West, Crystal Gayle, Larry Gatlin, Johnny Cash, Jerry Lee Lewis, Tom T. Hall, Vince Gill, Larnelle Harris, Bill Monroe, George Beverly Shea, Vestal Goodman, Bill Gaither, Connie Smith, DC Talk, Andrae Crouch, Commissioned, Vickie Winans, Ray Boltz, Steve Greene, and scores of others.

In 2001, Dottie received an ASCAP (American Society of Composers, Authors, and Publishers) lifetime achievement award. Christian Country Music Association honored her in 1994 as the Songwriter of the Century, and in 2002 presented her with the Living Legend award.

She is a member of the Southern Gospel Music Hall of Fame, and she has been inducted into the Gospel Music Hall of Fame twice, as a soloist and as part of the Rambo trio.

As hundreds gathered into the Ringgold United Methodist Church in Ringgold, Georgia, in 2007, it was a night when one of the legends came to help us kick off the Share America Foundation, Inc. and our Pearl and Floyd Franks Scholarship. There was electricity in the air as we welcomed her to the stage. While it was meant to be a solo engagement, before long as the show went on, we had added a bass, a fiddle, a banjo, a piano, and some talented harmony singers whose presence elated Dottie and actually infused her performance with even greater intensity.

I remember at one point in the evening, after we had done many of her standards, she looked over at me and asked if I had one of her songs I would like her to sing.

We had already done almost everything that was floating through my head as I stood on the spot, so in a moment of desperation I jok-

Stand By the River — Dottie Rambo

ingly said the only thing that came to mind — "The Old Grey Mule," hoping to get a laugh. It did, and without missing a beat, Dottie sang it adding the line, "This isn't very spiritual is it?"

Dottie prayed with me through some of my toughest periods as a caregiver, and she showed so much love and kindness to me. I will always miss this wonderful saint.

The world changed drastically the morning of Mother's Day 2008 as Dottie stepped into Heaven to be sheltered in the arms of God. She and her staff were in a tragic bus accident in Missouri that took Dottie dearest and injured all that were with her.

Prior to her passing, I had nominated Dottie for two honors because of the creative period in her life that she spent living in Georgia. She was inducted into the Atlanta Country Music Hall of Fame in 2007, but, due to injury, she was unable to attend and accept; so I had the honor of going on her behalf and sharing her acceptance speech.

The second was her induction into the Georgia Music Hall of Fame. Dottie was the first nomination I had made that sailed straight through in the first year of submission. She was inducted posthumously in the fall of 2008.

Ringgold City Councilmen Bill McMillon (right) and Tom Clark (second from right) join Randall Franks in honoring Dottie Rambo with Dottie Rambo Day in Ringgold, Georgia, on April 14, 2007.

© 2007 Randall Franks Media

Randall Franks — 1989

The King of the Southern Gospel Ivories, Hovie Lister

(In November 2001, I had the opportunity to sit down with the man who inspired my interest in the piano, the legendary Hovie Lister. This interview came shortly before his final quartet appearance on November 29 at the Colonnade near Ringgold in Catoosa County, Georgia. Hovie died December 28.)

When reviewing the history of America's gospel music, there are many great soldiers of ministry, but few have attained the status of a true legend and industry leader like Hovie Lister (1926–2001). With thousands of performances, awards, and experiences, he reminisces fondly.

Hovie Lister reviews his set list backstage November 29, 2001, at the Colonnade near Ringgold, Georgia.

"It's hard to look back on fifty years and single out one particular time that you have been in front of a crowd," Lister said. "I've had so many outstanding days, but if I started on something about the first time we were in Chicago, I'd also have to think about the first time we had the all-night to

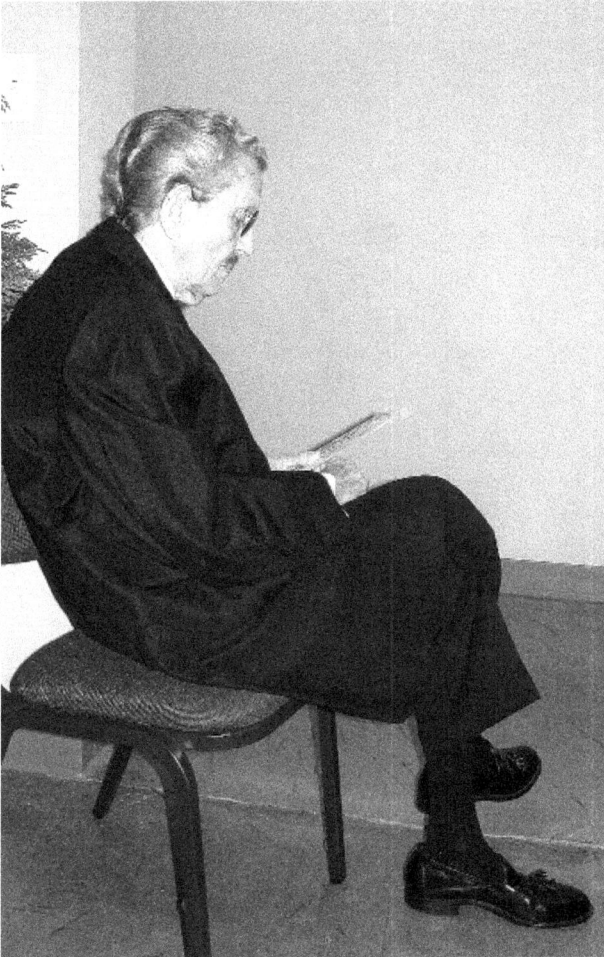

Encouragers

sunrise sing in Waycross, Georgia. It is just hard to single out one thing.

"Thankfully, I have enjoyed fifty-three years of wonderful relations with the public and people in the gospel music industry," he said. "One of the happiest times in my life was when I was pastoring a country church in Cobb County and still going every week with the Statesmen, and then getting back on Sunday morning in time to preach at Mt. Zion

Hovie Lister plays as Jack Toney lifts his voice in song.

The King of the Southern Gospel Ivories, Hovie Lister

Baptist Church. Being in Chicago and singing to a paid crowd of six thousand people then driving all night for preaching Sunday morning at that little country church and seeing all those wonderful folks was a real blessing."

Lister, who was an ordained Southern Baptist minister, was among the regulars appearing on Gaither videos and television broadcasts nationwide.

Hovie began to study music by taking piano lessons at age six. At fourteen, he was a pianist for song composer C. Austin Miles who authored "In The Garden." Miles and Hovie performed for evangelist Mordeca Ham.

After attending the Stamps Baxter School of Music, Hovie joined the Rangers Quartet and later the LeFevre Trio. In 1945, he became a pianist for the Homeland Harmony Quartet heard on WAGA and WGST Radio in Atlanta.

In 1948, a dream of Hovie's became a reality when he organized the world famous Statesmen at WCON.

Under the leadership of Lister, the Statesmen became the first gospel quartet to be featured on national TV syndication with a national sponsor, The National Biscuit Co., better known as Nabisco. He also led the Statesmen to appearances on NBC, ABC, and CBS as feature performers on the "Arthur Godfrey Show," "Tennessee Ernie Ford Show," and the "Jimmy Dean Show."

Of all the songs he wrote, Lister felt "Simply Hands" is the best.

He spent eighteen years with RCA and later Capitol Records, among other labels. His recordings have garnered eight Grammy nominations and one Grammy Award along with feature articles in several major publications.

Lister was inducted to the Georgia Music Hall of Fame, Southern Gospel Music Hall of Fame, and Gospel Music Hall of Fame — both individually and with the Statesmen.

He married Ethel Abbott of Lithonia. Their two children are Lisa and Chip.

Hovie said he was blessed with some of America's finest talent in the Statesmen. The Statesmen in 2001 were tenor singer Wallace Nelms, lead singer Jack Toney, baritone singer Rick Fair, and bass

Encouragers

singer Doug Young.

"I feel blessed all the way around," he said. "Wallace is a wonderful guy and a great singer, too. Jack is the top of the line. Bill Gaither said the other day that of all the lead singers of today that Jack Toney was probably the finest. Rick is one of the finest baritone voices in gospel music, and Doug is a fine Christian young man who is one of the best bass singers we have today."

Nelms, who is from Kingsport, Tennessee, has been with Hovie for eight years.

"Hovie (was) a master," Nelms said. "There were four masters in gospel music that you could put in that category. Hovie Lister, James Blackwood, J.D. Sumner, and Brock Speer. That has been the core of gospel music for forty years. Of course, it is changing now."

"Never has there been anyone who has done so much to make gospel music exciting," said Dove Award winner Phil Cross after Hovie's death.

© 2001 Randall Franks Media – Randall Franks

Hovie Lister takes one last bow.

158

Sure Nuff Singing — The Dixie Melody Boys

When it comes to straight-ahead Southern gospel music, there are none that are quite like the Dixie Melody Boys. In 2006, I had the pleasure of talking in length to the group's leader, Ed O'Neal:

"I started in this thing early in life, and it was different than the old Blackwood Brothers, Statesmen style singing," he said. "I have not done any of that in a lot of years."

Performance styles have changed through the years from the use of bands to soundtracks.

"We still do some soundtracks in the programs, but we do a good fifteen- to twenty-minute segment of just the old stuff," he said. "That goes over so good. We don't have a band. We will have a piano player, but the piano plays with tracks when we use tracks."

Ed O'Neal pauses for a photo on Dollywood's Red Carpet while walking to the 2010 Singing News Awards and SGMA Inductions.

He said that the trend of using musical sound tracks has changed the face of the music.

"Years ago, you couldn't have done it," he said. "I remember the Blackwood Brothers were the first I heard to really do it. It was really looked down on, but with the economy like it, is, it's almost impossible to have a four-piece band to travel.

"If groups use tracks right, it's fantastic because you get the entire orchestra," he said. "A lot (of performers) are not experienced in it,

159

and they will have the tracks loud and you just can't hear the singing. We do real well in it."

The legendary singer said he sees the industry as being bigger and better than ever.

"One reason is we've got so many doing it now," he said. "Back in the old days when you left the Blackwoods, Statesmen, LeFevres, and the Speer Family, the rest were almost unheard of. Now we got them on every corner."

While their music is a mainstay on Southern gospel radio, and they travel from Kinston, North Carolina, O'Neal said their group has made their performance mark outside the South.

"We started in the North when I got started in it," he said. "I didn't feel like we needed anybody else in the South. We made inroads there all the way to New England. Since about 1987, we spread out to the West, including the west coast."

He said he was greatly surprised by his induction into the Southern Gospel Music Hall of Fame in 2004.

"It never crossed my mind that I'd be included with my heroes — Hovie (Lister) and George Younce, Glen Payne, and James Blackwood," he said. "When they called me, it was just the thrill of my life because you know when you're in the Hall of Fame and that bronze head is there that your grandchildren's grandchildren will see it one day."

Despite his Hall of Fame induction, he points to receiving the Marvin Norcross Award in 2000 as his greatest experience. As an executive for Word Music which established Canaan Records, Norcross was an industry leader who brought Southern gospel to mainstreet America in the 1960s-70s. He was an active Rotarian and leader in the Little League Baseball in Texas.

"Marvin Norcross was a great man in our industry, and they named a humanitarian award in his honor," he said. "That was a total surprise. I was sitting there with my wife, tie undone, just relaxing watching the groups on award night, and all of a sudden they are talking about that. They called me up, and I was totally unprepared."

No matter how you sum up a visit with Ed O'Neal, it is safe to say that you can see a true love of God in what he does in life. I encourage you to find out more, by visiting www.dixiemelodyboys.com.

Jimmy Jones

(I interviewed Southern Gospel Music Hall of Fame member Jimmy Jones (1921–2006) in October 2002.)

After fifty-eight years on the road, Jones said the focus of his shows has not changed much.

"The idea is the same — spreading the gospel and singing

Randall Franks and Jimmy Jones

about our Lord, Jesus Christ," he said. "Since (the early days), the technology has changed considerably. Now the groups do more work in churches than we did. Back then, concerts were basically given in city and school auditoriums.

"I think back then (performances) leaned a little bit more to entertainment than it does now," he said. "I think that in our minds, every group would strive to entertain but also hopefully sow a seed and give a message that will be of help."

Jones, who regularly appears in the Bill Gaither gospel video series, began a full-time career in gospel music in 1944.

"I think Gaither videos have been the greatest boost that gospel singing has had in a long time," he said. "It has practically kept Southern gospel music alive the last several years. I have nothing but praise for Bill's work. He is a great man."

The early years

As did most gospel groups in the forties, Jones performed on radio and traveled within the boundaries of the station's signal to make live appearances promoting the songbooks.

"(When I started), practically every group worked with a music company," he said. "I started out with Hartford Music Company in Hot Springs, Arkansas, performing with Otis Echols and the Melody Boys."

161

Encouragers

"On weekends, we made singing conventions and sold our song-books," he said. "We were in competition with Stamps-Baxter publishing company.

"Everybody that made a living in music had an early morning radio program," he said. "Of course, everything was live. We sang nearly every night, but it was only one group. The only time we sang with other groups was at the singing conventions."

Jones moved to KWKH in Shreveport, Louisiana, where he based his performing from 1945-48.

"I moved there with the Melody Boys," he said. "We disbanded the quartet and organized a Western Swing band and did rodeos. I also went with a regular orchestra for two to three years."

He went to Los Angeles, California, and performed for a couple of years before moving to Texas in 1950 where he joined the Rangers Quartet.

"They were some of the greatest guys in the world," he said. "They were true professionals."

After three years, he decided to move on once again.

"Denver Crumpler and I left the Rangers, and he went to the Statesmen, and I came to Atlanta and organized the Deep South Quartet," he said.

For three years, Jones headed the Deep South Quartet.

"We worked in Washington, D.C., on television with Jimmy Dean," he said. "My brother had to quit singing for health reasons, and we left the Jimmy Dean show, and I disbanded the group and went to the LeFevres."

The LeFevres

Jones is perhaps best remembered for his "Poetry Corner" segment on the popular "Gospel Singing Caravan" television program, which featured the LeFevres, the Blue Ridge Quartet, the Prophets, and the Johnson Sisters.

"We did our taping part of the time in Charlotte, part of the time in Atlanta, a few times in Birmingham and Chattanooga," he said. "The four groups toured together."

Jones performed with the LeFevres for eleven years from 1957-68.

162

Jimmy Jones

"We were on television in forty-eight markets across the U.S.," he said. "We had ten years where it was Eva Mae and Urias and Uncle Alf, Pierce, Rex Nelon, and myself. I think we probably did some of the finest work we have ever done."

Gospel Music Hall of Famer and Grammy winner Eva Mae LeFevre remembered fondly the time Jones spent with the group and how happy he always was.

"Jimmy Jones was one of the few men we ever hired that really knew how to travel," she said. "When he was with us, he was a baritone singer, and he was one of the best baritones that I thought was around."

LeFevre said Jones carried a lot of the load when he worked with their group.

"He was one of the most honest men I have ever known," she said. "If you had a million dollars, you could trust him with it. That is how much faith I had in him and still do to this very day."

The Heralds

Some years ago, Jones joined with four men to create the Heralds with whom he sang bass. Hal Medlin was on tenor, David Morrison on lead, Steve Davis on baritone, and Charles Key playing piano. The group, except for Key, met as members of the Mt. Harmony Baptist Church choir in Mableton, Georgia.

Key also began his illustrious career in gospel music in 1944. He was the original pianist for the Harmoneers Quartet during their eighteen-year reign at the top of the gospel music charts in the 1950s and sixties.

He was inducted in to the Georgia Music Hall of Fame in September 2002 as a member of the Harmoneers.

"The Lord has been awfully good to me," Jones said. "I would not want to have done anything else. I enjoy life more than anybody you have ever saw."

Jimmy was inducted posthumously into the Southern Gospel Music Hall of Fame in 2007.

I was honored to have known Jimmy and be encouraged by elements of his work from throughout his career.

163

Randall Franks — 1989

The Greatest Bass Singer of Them All

I often find myself on a marathon trying to update my scrapbooks. Often, when we think of scrap it is something we wish to discard. If I don't get all this stuff organized and put away that is likely what its destiny will be.

As I look over the additions to the books I often refer to as my performance legacy, there are so many events and places already forgotten in the endless list of appearances and happenings.

As I recently ran across a photo of George Younce (1930–2005) standing at a microphone in the studio, I was reminded of an experience that for me was one of the greatest honors of my musical career.

For those who are not familiar with Southern gospel music, George Younce and Glen Payne were the hinge pins of the Cathedral Quartet that launched its career working with evangelist Rex Humbard in the 1960s.

George Younce sings in Perfection Sound Studios in Smyrna, Georgia, in 1987.

© 1987 Randall Franks Media – Randall Franks

The Cathedrals were probably the greatest male quartet of the latter quarter of the twentieth century.

Their music is timeless, and if the Cathedrals introduced a song it was almost destined to become a standard. The list is endless, but some tunes that struck a fire in my soul are "Step into the Water,"

Encouragers

"Champion of Love" (written by Ringgold's Phil Cross), and "I Just Started Living."

I remember when I was recording with the Marksmen we were so enthused when we took the popular Cathedrals song "Can He, Could He, Would He" and turned it into an instrumental featuring fiddle, guitar, and mandolin for our "Back to Basics" release. It became one of our more popularly requested instrumentals because of the way we mirrored the instruments to play off one another throughout the melody.

Without the Cathedrals, so many of today's Southern gospel performers, who worked with the group might not have found an introduction to gospel fans — Gerald Wolfe, Roger Bennett, Kirk Talley, and Danny Funderburk, among others.

© 2011 Randall Franks Media – Randall Franks

Gerald Wolfe and Gordon Mote host the Singing News Fan Awards in 2011.

I was working for MBM Records, headquartered in Smyrna, Georgia, back in 1987 as director of sales and promotions. Within that capacity, I worked closely with the artists in development of their products and careers.

We were working on what in the trade is called a custom project; one made by the artist with his own funds rather than by the record company.

George's son-in-law, Robbie Willis, who played drums for the Rex Nelon Singers, was doing a solo project. His father-in-law graciously agreed to sing on the project.

I had the honor of playing fiddle on it and assisting with the cover

166

The Greatest Bass Singer of Them All

design. I believe Kent Morris engineered that project. Of course, Steve Easter could have had a hand in it as well.

I'll never forget the excitement that I felt to know that the great bass voice of George Younce would be coming into our studio to record. Everything had to be just right.

We had worked hard preparing everything so he could overdub his part without a great deal of distraction.

I remember sitting in the control room as the melodious tones just rolled with ease off his golden vocal chords. Between takes, he would crack a light joke to help keep things moving.

I took several photos during his visit and enjoyed talking with him briefly about his experiences.

To get to record on an album with him and also play a part in making that project come to fruition was monumental for me.

I did not have a chance to speak with George again except in passing at the quartet convention, but when I saw him on the Gaither gatherings I felt as if I am watching an old friend.

As I look back on the pieces of my career, I am blessed that God allowed our paths to cross and the gifts God shared with us in our artistry to intertwine on a project.

Now the God of patience and consolation grant you to be likeminded one toward another according to Christ Jesus:

Romans 15:5

© 1990 Randall Franks Media – Ned D. Burris

Randall Franks — 1990

Dixie Echoes Solidifying the Future with the Past

As I stood off stage listening to the amazing artistry of the singers and the piano player, I was carried back to the days when I was traveling with The Marksmen Quartet when I would stand backstage and watched one of the groups that helped me form my tastes in gospel music.

From the earliest days of watching television, I had seen the Dixie Echoes in my family's living room. I still remember the day we got to where we could buy a second TV so we could have one sitting in the kitchen. One of the main reasons was so we could watch it while we ate breakfast getting ready to go to church.

What was playing? "The Gospel Singing Jubilee." So, in that respect I was always excited whenever I saw that we were on the bill with Randy Shelnut and his entire group. His late father Dale Shelnut initially led the group, and Randy carries on the tradition with his son Randy Jr. or "Scoot" by his side.

Today the group is concentrating on stepping into the future with the past firmly being part of what they are doing.

It's not unusual to see them walk out four men and a piano and sing, sing, sing until the audience begs for more.

"It started at Grand Ole Gospel Reunion," Randy Sr. said in a 2007 interview. "They have one night where all the groups have to sing like that.

"As we did it, I realized it's not only more fun, it makes you more of a team," he said. "You can feel the power in the songs. In thirty-eight years, I've never felt the power of the songs more than we do now."

They don't have to worry about folks complaining it's too loud. They only think about how the words are affecting those sitting in front of them and working to share with them the sharpest harmonies earnestly delivered.

"I think it's more because you feel the message in the song and are not distracted by something in the background," he said. "I feel like it is very true if the singer does not feel the song then the audience is not going to feel it either.

"I'm positive our music is not for everyone," he said. "The bulk of

169

Encouragers

people who want Southern gospel don't want the PA systems too loud. When groups do go that route, it seems to be exactly the opposite of what people want."

One of my favorites of their CDs is "Sounds of Sunday." The group shares some of the most pleasant, uplifting performances that I've heard. Listening to the CD, I can see them on stage. The collection is non-stop joy from the first note of "If Jesus Is There" to the last sounds of "After the Sunrise" fade away.

Abner, Abernathy, Brumley, Baxter, and Wright are some of the famous hymn writers who were included with songs such as "Up to the House of Prayer," "I Won't Have to Worry," "New Born Feeling," "Ole Brother Noah," "If We Never Meet Again," "The Last Mile of the Way," and "Praise the Name of God."

Since that project some seven years ago, the group has continued to pour out their hearts in similar fashion in release after release. I am also partial to their "Wonderful Days" CD, which came out in 2014.

Randy said he believes that audiences are primed for the straightforward approach they are presenting.

"I've seen it before in the early 70s," he said. "That's when a lot of the groups like the Inspirations and much later the McKameys rose to prominence. Those groups' successes were a direct product of folks being at a similar point to where they are now. They don't really care for what is going on in the industry now.

"The groups that did provide that feel a simple arrangement of powerful songs is what people are drawn to," he said. "That is why I see our popularity increasing dramatically."

He said that so much of the industry is now tied to soundtracks, but live music provides an entirely different experience.

"We have to bear in mind what our music is and what fits it," he said. "It is like taking jazz and putting a distortion guitar in it. Let the words and vocal be predominant."

The quartet also includes tenor Ben Hart, Alex and Andrew Utech, and Junior Shelton.

For more information, visit dixieechoes.com.

Pickin' and Grinnin' Friends
Rock 'n' Roll Music

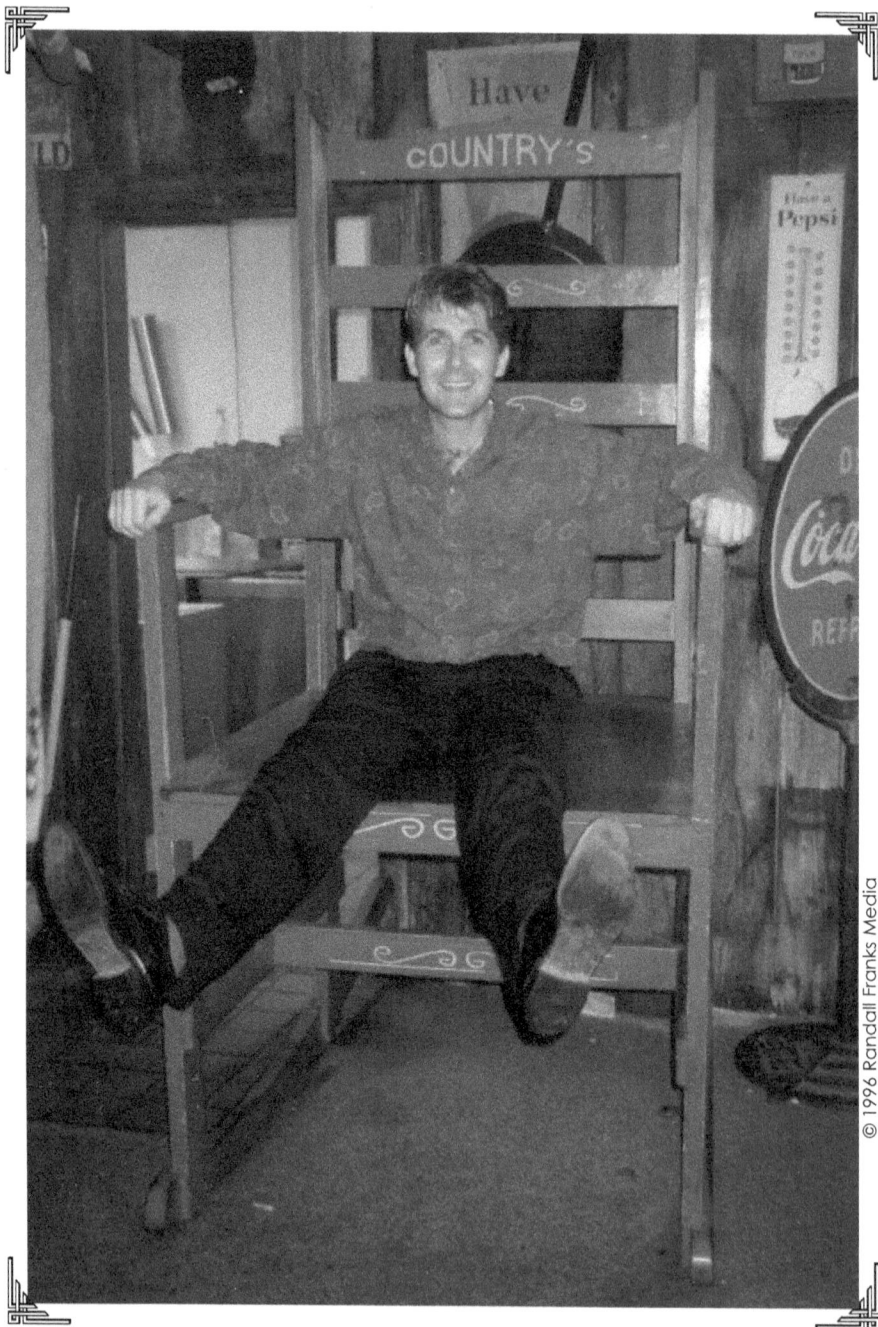

Rockin' Randall Franks — 1996

The Amazing Mae Axton

One of the most unique individuals that I ever had the pleasure of meeting and working with is Mae Boren Axton (1914–1997). Many in the public might not know her name, but for those of us who have spent any time in Nashville, she is one of music's royalty. To those who knew her, she was Mama Mae.

As a writer, she has the distinction of writing Elvis's "Heartbreak Hotel" with the late Tommy Durden.

In Florida, she was a teacher who, in her spare time, wrote for publications like Time and Life magazines. An assignment placed her smack dab in the middle of what was then called "hillbilly" music as her editors sent her to Nashville to do a feature in the early 1950s, where she did interviews with folks such as Minnie Pearl and Roy Acuff. That fateful assignment would place her in a position that would make her one of the best-known behind-the-scenes people in the entertainment world.

As an entertainer or songwriter, to reach any

© 1992 Randall Franks Media

Randall Franks with Mae Boren Axton backstage at TNN's "Nashville Now" following an appearance by Randall prior to his 1992 CBS musical debut on "In the Heat of the Night."

173

Encouragers

level of success, a performer has to pay their dues in Nashville, becoming a part of what makes up the musical fabric of the town.

During the period in my life when I was spending a great deal of time pursuing a mainstream music record deal, Mama Mae became one of my biggest allies and cheerleaders.

She had forged a career in publicity, promoting some of country music's greatest stars such as Hank Snow, Dolly Parton, Willie Nelson, and Porter Wagoner, as well as Hollywood's films.

She taught me that there is no one you cannot reach if you know how to do it. In my life, I have found that to be true. She once shared with me a story of how she managed to reach one of the biggest magazine publishers in the country and convince him to pull a story on Porter Wagoner minutes before it was to go to press.

Following a performance I did at an Ernest Tubb Record Shop Fan Appreciation Dinner, I met Mama Mae and she invited me to meet with her at her office. As president of DPI records in Nashville, she brought me in, and we discussed adding me to the label's roster.

At the time, DPI was one of the most visible independents labels. I would join Mae's son Hoyt Axton and rising DPI recording artist Mario Martin on the label.

Before the deal could be solidified, Mama Mae's doctors encouraged her to retire. She suggested I not make the deal with DPI and she would continue to help me.

She continued working with me until she passed away in 1997.

Whenever I was in Nashville, her door was always open to me. Her beautiful home reflected elegance and countless memories. Her walls were covered with awards, honors, and photos of her favorite people. Walking through the halls was like visiting the Country Music Hall of Fame. It chronicled her career from her earliest images with Elvis, Roger Miller, Bill Monroe, Garth Brooks, Reba McEntire, and so many others. When I stayed at her house, I never knew who might be bunking in the room next door, from Milton Berle to Dennis Weaver.

She always kept me in the forefront of what was happening in Nashville, making sure that label heads, producers, and other stars knew what I was up to.

The Amazing Mae Axton

Randall Franks and Hoyt Axton
visit at CMA Fan Fair June 6, 1990.

Mae would make sure when something important was happening I would be a part of it. She made arrangements for me to appear on Ralph Emery's Nashville Now just before my network musical debut.

In 1996, while I was living in California, Mae went to the Mayo Clinic. While visiting the offices of the Academy of Country Music in Hollywood, former ACM director Fran Boyd called her to wish her well. I joined in by playing "Orange Blossom Special" on the fiddle over the speakerphone to cheer her up.

On my last visit with her just days before she passed away, I arranged for her to attend Jim and Jesse's fiftieth anniversary celebration being held at the Grand Ole Opry. I escorted her to the event, and we had a wonderful evening visiting with friends.

That weekend, she was especially supportive of my writing as we sat in her office and went over my recent endeavors. She encouraged me to continue to use my talents no matter what opportunities were ahead of me. In many ways, I think she knew her time was near. She took the time to share many stories with me that she said she hoped someone would remember. One thing she wanted to share with me was an original disc jockey platter of "Heartbreak Hotel." Since she was not feeling well, I told her we could go down to the basement and get it next visit. Unfortunately, that did not happen.

She arranged her memorial service in advance down to every detail. Ralph Emery hosted; Sandy Brooks, Garth's former wife spoke; her grandchildren sang. While I sat in the church before the services, flowers, the original draft of "Heartbreak Hotel" and a large photo of her and Elvis surrounded her. As I waited there, several stars arrived to pay their respects, including Jim Ed Brown and Helen Cornelius. Lee Greenwood came in from his theater. I remember well the tears he shed as we talked near her casket. Sitting there was like looking at a who's who gathering of music. During the service, I sat next to Steve Wariner, and I believe Gail Davies or Victoria Shaw. After the service, she had planned a catered dinner at the Axton mansion. I remember Tanya Tucker looking endlessly at Mae's photo gallery. I shared with Hoyt how much Mama Mae had meant to me and how the mansion was a second home for me in Nashville. He told me that as long as he lived, it would be my Nashville home.

So many lives were touched and so many careers were pushed along gently by the loving presence of Mama Mae.

> *And Jesus stood still, and commanded him to be called. And they call the blind man, saying unto him, Be of good comfort, rise; he calleth thee.*
>
> **Mark 10:49**

Pick It Perkins — Carl Perkins

The Grammy award-winning 1987 recording "The Class of '55" linked in the minds of another generation, a group of entertainers cultivated by the late Sam Phillips in Memphis.

Johnny Cash, Jerry Lee Lewis, Carl Perkins, Roy Orbison and Elvis changed the face of American music as they fused the sounds of rhythm and blues from the Mississippi Delta with the sounds of country and western and pop, creating what became rock n' roll.

When my manager, Jeff Goodwin, called to say I was to co-host a special tribute to one of these legends, I was so excited.

One of my favorite forty-five records growing up was a Sun recording of Carl Perkins (1932–1998) singing "Blue Suede Shoes" and "Honey Don't."

Released on New Years Day 1956, the copy I listened to over and over was created by Plastics Products in Memphis and dispatched by Sun Records to place in jukeboxes around the country.

Beginning in early 1956, this copy spun repeatedly in my mother's restaurant, Robinson's Café, on Oak Street in downtown Chattanooga, as teens and adults dropped their nickels and dimes into that old jukebox.

The event was a black tie gathering featuring a special performance by Carl in his home of Jackson, Tennessee. Not only would I get to perform on stage with Carl, but also I was to co-host the event with "Dukes of Hazzard" and "Enos" star Sonny Shroyer, whom I watched on television religiously while growing up.

Both Sonny and I arrived at the event early and visited with Carl. We all were to perform in front of a symphony orchestra that evening.

Carl appeared much as I expected him. He arrived in blue jeans and a plain shirt as he greeted each of us.

I told him what an honor it was to be a part of the evening, and brought along my forty-five for him to autograph.

He did it without hesitation, while saying autographed original copies of his first million-seller sell for a premium.

He took the time to sit down and tell me how he wrote the song while he and his wife, Val, were living in public housing.

He said he had performed at a dance the night before and noticed a

177

Encouragers

Randall Franks, Carl Perkins, and Sonny Shroyer share the stage in Jackson, Tennessee, in 1996.

man out on the dance floor trying to keep his girlfriend from stepping all over his shoes.

At around three the next morning, he rose out of bed and went to the kitchen looking for something to write on. All he had was an old potato sack. He sat down and in just a few minutes wrote out in pencil the words that had come to him.

He said Val came out to see what he was doing, and he handed her the song. After she read it, he said she knew right then that it was going to be a hit.

While I was excited about just meeting and getting to perform with Carl, my managers had another goal up their sleeve. At the time, they hoped two possibilities might arise from the meeting. I understand at the time that Disney was negotiating with Carl for the rights to his story for the movie to be called "Go Cat Go!"

My managers, with Carl's circle of advisors, were pushing for me to play the icon in the film. Since Carl was to retain creative control, including casting approval, my managers told me that my possibility of playing the role was very strong. Alas, the film never materialized. It would have been a blast to portray one of the class of '55.

They also hoped that a couple of songwriting sessions might develop from the meeting, but, due to various conflicts on both our parts, neither of us were able to make that ever come to pass either, although

Pick It Perkins — Carl Perkins

we stayed in touch throughout the remainder of his life.

That night in Jackson, Sonny and I walked on stage in front of a packed house and bantered back and forth. We brought the house down with our country jokes and guided the evening of music and accolades for Carl with almost seamless precision.

As the evening came to a close, I rushed back stage, quickly tightened up my bow, and tucked my fiddle up under my arm. It seemed I did not even have time to get nervous. As soon as the instrument was in hand, Carl brought me back out on stage. I took my position as the conductor rose his baton. Carl looked over, smiled, and gazed back out into the audience. It seemed that that moment was endless almost in slow motion.

There I was standing in the shadow of the first entertainer to cross over in all the fields of chart music of the fifties, rhythm and blues, and pop and country. He was a performer, who, if not for a twist of fate on the way to appear on the Perry Como Show when he was sidelined for months after a car accident, could have beat fellow '55 classmate Elvis out of his first RCA number one, "Heartbreak Hotel," at least for a while.

As I anxiously watched him, it seemed he just soaked up the love given by the audience as they waited in anticipation for the hit that had spun on my old beige portable turntable more times than I could count.

Like an explosion from a cannon, the words flowed from his mouth, "It's one for the money," as easily as they did upon that old potato sack decades before. The conductor moved his baton and we struck the chords. We did not stop until the audience was on its feet begging for more.

In my mind, I was begging, too. I hated for that evening to end, but the little things he showed me about his music are still a part of what I do each time I walk on stage.

© 1992 Randall Franks Media – J. Alan Palmer

Randall Franks — 1992

Haven't I Seen You on Television?

Lights, Camera, Action Friends

Randall Franks — 1990

Carroll O'Connor

Randall Franks and Carroll O'Connor
on the set of "In the Heat of the Night."

When I was just beginning my career as an actor and really just beginning my adulthood, Carroll O'Connor (1927–2001) came into my life. Growing up, I had watched him faithfully as "Archie Bunker" on "All in the Family."

When "In the Heat of the Night" began airing in its pilot season, I was amazed at how he took on the role of a Southern police chief and made the character so real. I remember my first day on the set like it was yesterday. The August heat was heavy on the skin as we gathered for the first day on location, filming in Georgia. Casting director Dee Voight called me the night before and asked me to come in to be an extra. She thought that there might be some future for me on the show.

Most of the actors had flown in on the red-eye from Los Angeles the night before. I remember seeing Carroll — "Pops," as I would later call him. I was in awe of this television icon. I was so afraid I might embarrass myself in front of him. The scene we shot included all of the cast and around twenty extras. One of the rules of working on a film or show is not to speak to the stars unless they speak to you. At one point during the day, three of us were singled out to do a short bit with

Encouragers

Carroll coming out of the woods as he headed for his car. Standing there in the woods waiting for action, I had my first conversation with this acting icon. I had watched him in awe most of the day.

In that first encounter, he spoke with the three of us in his Chief Gillespie accent: "Y'all young folks don't do any drugs do you? The Lord wouldn't want you to do drugs." I guess it was a way for him to break the tension to help us feel at ease around him.

For him, this was a message he would eventually share with the world after his son Hugh took his own life as a result of drug use in 1995.

The Lord blessed my life in opening an opportunity for me at "In the Heat of the Night." Through Carroll, he created many of those opportunities for me. While the original producers gave me the job, it was Carroll that gave me the words to say again and again as well as so many interesting tasks to do. He stood up for me and told the networks and the studios that he felt I could do the job. For him, I did my best, and for him, I would still try to move mountains.

In many ways he became a father figure for me shortly after the death of my own father. He gave me guidance in so many ways. Like a father and son, we did not always see eye-to-eye on everything, but because of him, I have enjoyed many experiences in my life. Because he had shared his knowledge and friendship with me, I am a much better person.

When he had his heart surgery during the show, there was a tremendous void on the set. I feared that he might not return as rumors of possible replacements flew. But he did return, and in the process took over and became executive producer. The Sparta, Mississippi, of our series would not have been the same without him.

The quiet times we shared just sitting on the front porch in a sleepy Southern town watching the world go by will always be some of my favorites times with him — hearing his stories about various things he had done, his last visit with John Wayne, his work on numerous shows and movies, mistakes he had made, and things that he never thought would fly but did, like "All in the Family."

In 1990, Carroll agreed to be a part of a Christmas CD, "Christmas

Carroll O'Connor — 1990

Carroll O'Connor

Time's A Comin'" that Alan Autry and I produced to raise funds for drug abuse prevention charities. As producer, I then got to switch places with Carroll for a short time and be his boss — so to speak. I was privileged to get to produce his song "Bring A Torch, Jeanette Isabella." He wanted it to be unique. I think we, along with some great musicians, accomplished that.

Television, my life, and the world would not be the same without all Carroll O'Connor shared with us. He blessed us with laughter, hope, and a different view on how life could be if we only tried to make a difference. I miss him as I did when my role on the show came to an end. His lovely wife, Nancy, also shared much kindness with me during our association. He and Nancy welcomed my late mother Pearl and I into their home to share the holidays. What a wonderful memory we created together that I still look upon fondly.

I thank God for letting me be part of his "Heat" family. It is a unique group of people from which we have already lost too many members.

While many will see him forever as "Archie Bunker," to me he will always be "Pops," our "Chief." I can still hear him telling Parker "Get Randy some backup."

That's what he did for people — backed them up. Many have asked me if Carroll was a good guy to work with.

All I can say is, "Sho nuff, Chief, Sho nuff."

With whom my hand shall be established: mine arm also shall strengthen him.

Psalm 89:21

The Day I Didn't Meet Andy Griffith

It was during a hiatus of "In the Heat of the Night" that I made my very first trip to Hollywood. Graciously, the former director of photography of our show, the late Peter Salim (1939–1994), offered me a couch to sleep on during my time there. Actors often rely on other folks in the business to put them up while they are in Los Angeles auditioning or looking for an agent. This is a time-honored custom, since in many cases the host may want to ask the guest for a job at some point in the future when they do get their break.

I was trying to secure a new agent and hoping to maybe audition for a project or two while I was there. Peter was working as direc-

Randall Franks and Peter Salim in front of Grauman's Chinese Theater in Hollywood.

© 1992 Randall Franks Media

tor of photography on "Murder, She Wrote," and while I was there he was directing an episode. (A director of photography runs the camera while a director runs the actors.)

Since the 1970s, Peter had worked his way up through the ranks in the camera department. He was second camera operator on "All the President's Men," where he also played the part of a reporter. He was the camera operator on "The Lost Boys" in 1987, and by the time he accepted a job with "Spencer: For Hire" he was director of photography. While at "In the Heat of the Night," he made the jump to being a

187

director. He always included me in his episodes of "In the Heat of the Night," and I imagine if this episode of "Murder, She Wrote" had not been set in England, I would have had a shot at that. I did, however,

get to spend several days on the set in between my appointments.

While there, I also called on another director friend, the late Leo Penn (1921–1998), father of Sean, Michael, and Christopher Penn. Leo had directed several of our shows and was also some-one that was always in my corner. He was also work-ing at the Universal lot directing "Matlock." He was shooting an episode that would be Randy

Randall Franks and Leo Penn on the set.

© 1992 Randall Franks Media

Travis' debut on the show. Timing is everything in television. Mine seemed to be off this trip.

As I visited the set of "Murder, She Wrote" — another one of my favorite shows — the star, Angela Lansbury, was not working. However, I met her son, the director. When Leo invited me to the set of "Matlock," I met all the other stars, such as Clarence Gilyard, and Nancy Stafford, who is still a friend. Andy Griffith (1926–2012) was not working, and I did not get to meet him then.

It would have been a wonderful chance to be introduced to him by a director that he respected like Leo and maybe, just maybe, get a chance at a role later, but it did not happen. Later, while returning from the Universal commissary from lunch to the set of "Murder, She Wrote" with Peter, who should we happen to come up to but Andy Griffith. He was standing outside his trailer, talking with some crew members. I was maybe three feet away.

The Day I Didn't Meet Andy Griffith

Peter looked over at me and said, "Don't do it." He knew what a fan I was of Andy, and even though he knew I was a professional, he wanted to reinforce my thinking process. Of course, he might have also envisioned an "I Love Lucy" type of celebrity encounter as well. Everyone remembers what a disaster Lucy made out of meeting stars.

So, I did not walk up to Andy and introduce myself. I did not tell him what an effect he had on my life.

That trip showed me I had a lot to learn about being an actor. Even though I was a working actor, I still needed a tremendous amount of study so that I would feel comfortable to work on the level of these greats.

"In the Heat of the Night" in many ways had spoiled me because in so many ways it was like a home to me. There was a place for me there to fall down creatively in front of big stars and get back up to try again. It was the closest thing to the studio system of old that my generation will ever know.

But if I was to do anything else, I had to go out and carve a niche for myself elsewhere. That's not an easy task to leave but I did. Though I never officially met Andy Griffith, I was deeply saddened by his passing. I did get the opportunity some years later to share my written thanks to him for all the inspiration he shared with me. I still sit down almost every evening and spend thirty minutes with the character he created long before I was born — Andy Taylor. I will always have him as a friend each time I step back into the TV world of Mayberry, North Carolina.

In my time on the TV and movie sets and music stages, I have continued to learn from the entertainment greats that your time on the stage of fame and popularity may be fleeting, come and go with the whims of popular culture and the powers that be, but it's how you live your everyday life, how you treat those you meet, how you positively affect the people and world around you that really counts and makes you a star.

If I had met Andy that day years ago, I think that is the lesson he would have taught me. Andy Taylor imparted those same kinds of lessons to Opie. Thank you, Mr. Griffith!

© 1990 Randall Franks Media – Ned D. Burris

Randall Franks — 1991

Who Shot Who? — Larry Hagman

When I was in my youth, one actor was someone who had caught the fascination of three hundred million people around the world.

I joined them, wondering for a summer "Who Shot J.R.?"

Years later, I learned some of the behind-the-scenes wrangling being conducted as J.R. merchandise flew off the shelves helping to take "Dallas" from just a nighttime soap to a piece of Americana that would place its stars among the best-known actors in television history. Leading the way as one of the shows legends was Larry Hagman.

I had come to know Larry as the astronaut "Major Anthony Nelson" that found Barbara Eden's "Jeannie" on a beach and then spent years at her mercy as it were while pretending to be her master.

I officially met the actor Larry Hagman (1931–2012) after he was bringing his first run as "J.R. Ewing" to a close. He was a close friend to my boss and mentor Carroll O'Connor and so as part of his transition he came to "In the Heat of the Night" as a director under whom I was honored to act.

I found him to be a man truly searching to change the direction of

Randall Franks and Larry Hagman pause on the set of "In the Heat of the Night" in 1991.

Encouragers

his life and use his remaining time to be a positive force in the world.

In the intermittent times I was around him over the next couple of years, I saw him navigate a new direction that I believe ultimately gave him the opportunity to reach eighty-one years and to once again play "J.R." on the most recent TNT version of the series.

I came to know a man that would leave a waitress a tip that was four hundred percent of the bill. I came to know a man that when a child asked for an autograph, he would ask them for something in return. I would hear him say, "Give me a poem, a scripture, or a song in exchange." His thinking was that if the child had to earn it, then it would mean more to them. In his own way, he was encouraging the youth into not expecting something for nothing.

He was such a gracious director, encouraging the actors into being brave with their choices even when it might go against common practices on our set. I remember we had a very tight rein on us relating to changing dialogue without Carroll's approval.

In one of the scenes where I was featured, I remember a discussion about getting approval for a change Larry wanted to make. Out of respect to both of them, I will leave out the comment he made when someone said it needed to be run by Carroll, but needless to say in J.R. Ewing style, he simply did it his way.

While we visited, he shared with me many stories of his experiences on "Dallas," and his work on "I Dream of Jeannie" and even how he didn't do the reunion for "I Dream of Jeannie."

Larry went out of his way to be very supportive of me as an actor on the set. Even once he went home, if I called upon him for some assistance, a bit of advice, he wouldn't hesitate. He didn't mind me calling him at home. He even shared with me some time later that he had become a fan of my music.

Larry continued working because that's what he loved to do. If I had one regret, it is that I never got to work on screen with Larry. I am however extremely pleased to know that he was back playing "J.R." again in his last couple of years. I know he was having a ball.

It is easy to see that even today, he was still working to make a difference and in his last months, he had created the Larry Hagman

Foundation, an organization funding educational programs that promote fine arts and creative learning opportunities for economically disadvantaged children in Dallas, Texas.

I began my professional television career as a youth in Dallas as part of the cast of the "Country Kids TV Series," so I am especially excited to see the legacy that Larry created continue there.

I encourage you, if Larry Hagman ever brought you and your family one minute of joy or escape with his work that you will take the time to donate to this wonderful effort in memory of a great man, a tremendous friend, and a great encourager. Visit www.larryhagman.com to learn more about his efforts.

But Joshua the son of Nun, which standeth before thee, he shall go in thither: encourage him: for he shall cause Israel to inherit it.

Deuteronomy 1:38

Randall Franks — 1991

McCloud Riding to the Rescue

The image of Deputy Marshal Sam McCloud galloping to the rescue on horseback through the busy streets of New York City is indelibly burned into my memory. You just could not help but want to see McCloud come out on top, and you really knew he would.

In the 1970s, there were not many television drama choices that did not carry a viewer to the grimy dirty streets of urban America.

"McCloud," which starred Dennis Weaver (1924–2006), was to me a breath of fresh air.

The series, which placed western lawman Sam McCloud in the big city, was one of the finest uses of television's "fish out of water" concept that ever made its way to film.

Randall Franks and Dennis Weaver at Fan Fair in 1989.

Weaver's brilliant, funny and always touching performances earned him three Emmy nominations.

Millions either know Weaver from this character, his numerous movie and television appearances over four decades, or from his portrayal of "Chester Goode" on "Gunsmoke," TV's longest running drama, for which he won an Emmy in 1959.

I used to joke behind the scenes on "In the Heat of the Night" that Chester must have been the great-grandpa to my "Randy Goode" character. I found the unique stories created for "McCloud" entertaining and meaningful.

I met Dennis Weaver many years ago at International Country Music Fan Fair in Nashville when he made a promotional visit there. I had the chance to visit with him and have a photo snapped.

Several years after my time at "In the Heat of the Night," he and his lovely wife, Gerry, would be my next-door neighbors. We were both regular visitors to the Axton Arms. That is, whenever we were in

Encouragers

Nashville, we often stayed with music writing icon Mae Boren Axton, who wrote Elvis Presley's "Heartbreak Hotel."

On one of my trips, Dennis and Gerry were in town to do some music recording, and I was in doing some promotional appearances. We had the opportunity to visit, listen to music, watch a little basketball, and really just have a tremendous time.

I can still remember us all gathering hand-in-hand in Mae's backyard for a prayer as we all prepared to go on our separate ways.

When we lost our dear friend Mae, I would have the sad duty of sharing with Dennis and Gerry the news of her passing. While I hoped I might be of some comfort to them, it turned out to be more the other way.

Dennis continued acting with a starring role in the film "Submerged," and other films such as "The Virginian" with Bill Pullman and Diane Lane for TNT and "The Escape from Wildcat Canyon," one of my favorites, a movie about survival and friendship in a harsh mountain habitat.

He is also known for his efforts to improve the environment. He and Gerry built a beautiful home that is environmentally friendly near Ridgway, Colorado. This type of house, which uses tires, aluminum cans, and other recycled materials as a part of the structure, is called an Earthship. The house uses solar mass to conserve heat and solar power.

The Institute of Ecolonomics, a non-profit organization founded by Dennis and Gerry Weaver in 1993, has dedicated itself to bringing about change. The IOE demonstrates that creating a symbiotic relationship between a strong economy and a healthy ecology is the only formula for a sustainable future.

I considered Dennis a friend, and I believe he would say the same of me. Through the years, I have met a lot of Hollywood people. Some were the crème of the crop, others were not. I consider the Weavers to be some of the greatest.

For those who never met Dennis, I will say he was solid as a rock in character. He was someone you could depend upon. I know our country lost someone who really made a difference on and off the television screen when he took his final bow.

Happy Trails — Roy Rogers

Although the days of the singing cowboys on the silver screen and television had already passed when I was growing up, Roy Rogers (1911–1998) and Dale Evans (1912–2001) were huge stars to me.

I had the pleasure of visiting the original family museum in Victorville, California, several years ago on a trip to Hollywood.

I met Roy in passing at an appearance he made at the 1992 CMA Awards when he and Clint Black performed a duet of Vocal Event of the Year nominee "Hold On, Partner."

It was not until a 1996 stop at Victorville that I had the chance to spend a bit of quality time with this screen legend. I was on my way to Los Angeles to audition for a new show being created for Jeff Foxworthy when I stopped off to spend some time with Roy and Dusty at the museum. Unfortunately, Dale was hospitalized at the time.

I arrived the night before and stayed in the motel there in town. On American Movie Channel that night was featured the Roy Rogers and Dale Evans film "Don't Fence Me In."

I was amazed the next day to find out as I sat and watched the movie at the motel that Roy was doing the same thing at his house a couple of miles away.

When I arrived, I let the staff know I dropped by to visit with Roy if he had time. While I was looking around at the exhibits in the museum, Roy drove up from the house and came in to his office.

While on many days he would visit with patrons, this day his spirits were low due to Dale's illness, and he limited his visiting to just us.

We talked like old friends sharing stories about his movies and my work on television. He reminisced fondly about Dale, his family, his loving mother, and how he started in film.

He coached me to never forget the fans. "Once they see you as a star, you are theirs from that point on," he said.

Dusty brought in a custom-made Roy Rogers revolver. Roy looked it over and held it up, commenting on how heavy it was to his arm now that the years were adding up on the King of the Cowboys.

Before I left, Roy even let me wear his hat for a photo. It's little things like that that made him more than a King.

What amazed me about the museum at the time was the sheer vol-

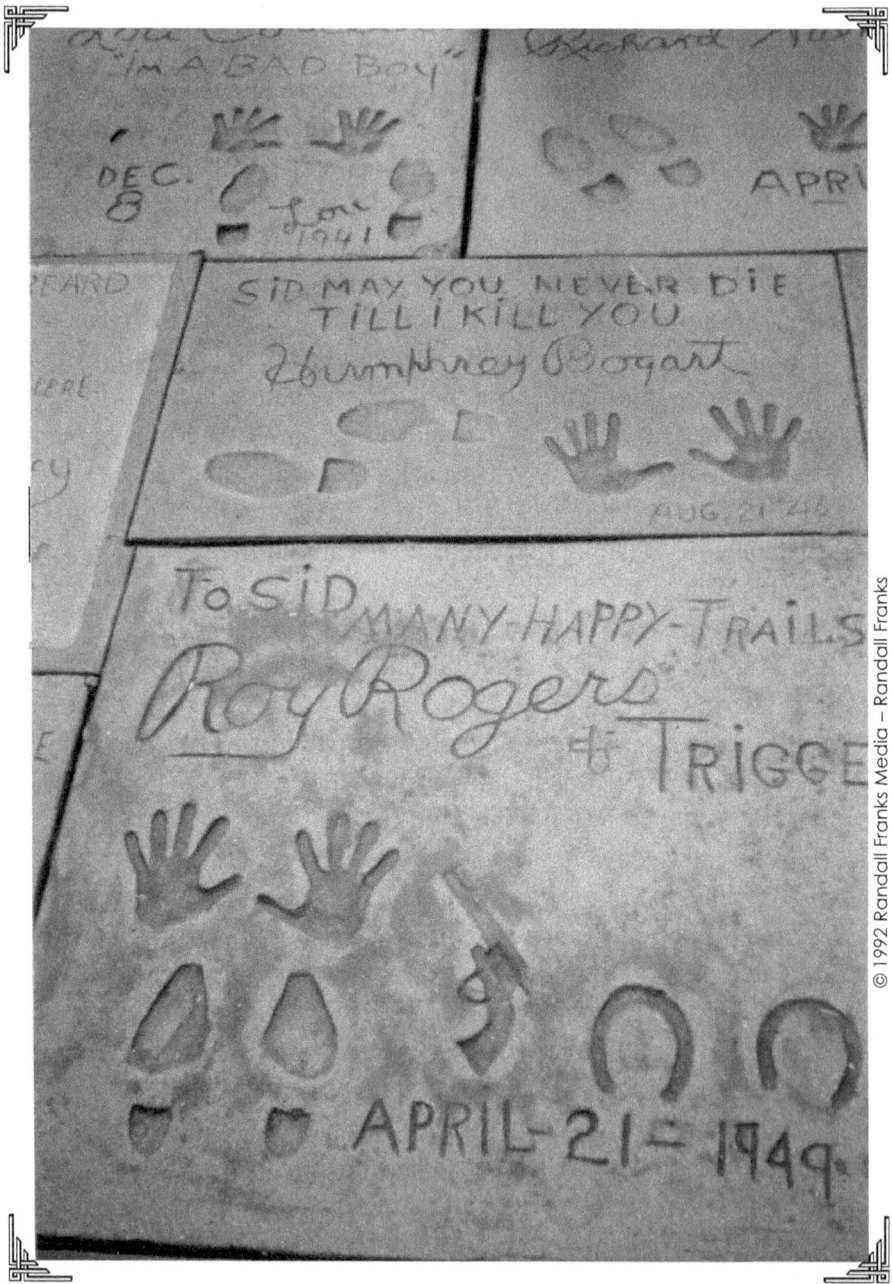

Grauman's Chinese Theater
Roy Rogers' and Trigger's footprints — 1992

Encouragers

Roy Rogers lets Randall Franks try his hat on for size in
Victorville, California, in 1996.

ume of material dating back to the earliest points in Leonard Slye's career.

It was all there from the truck his family traveled to California in to the little notes from famous and not so famous admirers.

Roy told me his mother saved a lot and encouraged him to save items as well.

Dusty has said his Dad could not bring himself to throw anything away. This trait made their museums an outstanding place to visit.

I saw two lifetimes of memorabilia, including Roy's steeds Trigger, Bullet, Buttermilk and Trigger, Jr.

The museum was a totally different experience.

Eventually, the family closed the Victorville museum and opened one in Branson, which thrived for a while. The museum collection was auctioned off in 2010. Roy "Dusty" Rogers, Jr. told me that his parents said when the collection started costing money to keep, it would be

Happy Trails — Roy Rogers

time.

Their musical legacy continues in the good hands of Roy Rogers, Jr. and his son Dustin Roy Rogers. They continue to keep the Rogers experience alive in America's heartland through their shows.

I visited their show in Branson in 2011, and I can assure you the time was a wonderful excursion into the western musical genre with a talented group of cowboys leading the way with the High Riders. Their musical abilities are tops, and they provide an enjoyable show that would leave any western fan

© 2011 Randall Franks Media – Randall Franks

Roy Rogers, Jr.

hankerin' for more.

Roy Jr. said the show continues to include the wonderful sounds that Roy Sr. made famous with the Sons of the Pioneers.

The 2012 Rose Parade featured a tremendous float highlighting the legacy of Roy and Dale with Roy Rogers, Jr. on board. The Rogers completed their final season at RFD-TV Theater in 2013. To find out the latest release from the Rogers, visit www.royrogersjr-show.com and www.royrogers.com.

© 2011 Randall Franks Media – Randall Franks

Dustin Rogers

"Rollin' Rollin' Rollin'" — Sheb Wooley

One of my former favorite Saturday afternoon diversions was to tune in to the Hallmark Channel and watch "Rawhide." The series launched the career of Clint Eastwood, but I look out for my friend Sheb Wooley (1921–2003), playing scout "Pete Nolan."

Sheb and I often reminisced about some of his adventures while working with Gary Cooper in "High Noon;" or James Dean, Rock Hudson, and Elizabeth Taylor in "Giant;" John Wayne and Kirk Douglas in "The War Wagon;" Errol Flynn in "Rocky Mountain;" or Gene Hackman in "Hoosiers."

Randall Franks and Sheb Wooley at CMA Fan Fair in 1994.

© 1994 Randall Franks Media – Donna Tracy

I met Sheb and his wife, Linda, in 1991. We were both appearing at the Celebrity Rose Classic Golf Tournament in Shreveport, Louisiana.

The three of us hit it off, and I was enthralled with Sheb's ability to entertain an audience as we did short programs at a gathering for the event sponsors. It was amazing to watch him perform his 1958 number one pop song "Purple People Eater," which has sold more than one hundred million copies.

Although "Rawhide" was not a show I got to see growing up, I have seen many of his movie roles, especially his riveting performance in "Hoosiers."

Sheb was a unique person who managed to keep both a unique recording career and an acclaimed film career afloat for decades. When trends changed in country music, he created his alter ego —

Encouragers

"Ben Colder" — to perform comedy songs. He was the 1968 Country Music Association Comedian of the Year. He became a regular on "Hee Haw" from its inception and wrote the show's theme song. No matter how he approached show business, Sheb scored numerous records that sold over a million copies and top-charting songs.

He began recording in 1945 for Bullet Records in Nashville and eventually signed with MGM Records for one of the longest tenures of any artist. He never stopped writing songs or trying to entertain, maintaining a tireless schedule of live appearances.

Sheb and Linda were kind enough to take me under their wing, adding me to the stable of talent they promoted through Dotson-Wooley Entertainment. With every movie project they pitched or television idea they created, I was thankful to be among those they included.

I often dropped by to see them in Nashville, and Sheb and Linda always welcomed me and made me feel a part of what they were doing.

Sheb often said, "Success lies in three things: dreams, hard work, and faith. You've got to dream the dream, do the work, and have the faith. Success can't resist that kind of formula."

Just as they helped me, I always tried to include Sheb in any project in which I might be involved, including trying to get him cast on "In the Heat of the Night." That was the way things once worked in Nashville and Hollywood — friends helped other friends keep growing and going.

All of the charities and fundraisers that celebrities lend their names to support is one aspect of life often overlooked when a celebrity passes. Sheb was someone who did not hesitate to help wherever he could.

Sheb's legacy lives on in his films and recordings. I just think of him as riding on ahead to scout out a path for us.

I hope to see him again when I reach the journey's end.

Head 'em up! Move 'em out!

Sheriff Lobo Serves Up Some Southern Sense

Growing up during a time when network television executives decided arbitrarily that any show that had a tree or a bale of hay in it should be canceled, getting to watch shows such as "The Waltons," "Dukes of Hazzard," "BJ and the Bear" and "The Misadventures of Sheriff Lobo" were a real treat.

One of my favorite short-lived series featured actor Claude Akins (1926–1994) as "Sheriff Lobo." Akins took up the Lobo character in 1978 in the "BJ and the Bear" series pilot with Greg Evigan and later went on to have his own spin-off series which ran from 1979–81.

While Lobo worked to get ahead by pulling some kind of scam working with "Deputy Perkins," played by Mills Watson, Brian Kerwin, who played "Deputy Birdie Hawkins," always managed to turn their underhanded scheme into an award-winning police bust. With each episode, Lobo just couldn't seem to get ahead financially with his underhanded plans as Hawkins kept making him look better and better.

Akins and Watson made up what could be one of the best classic tel-

Claude Akins and Randall Franks visit on the set of "In the Heat of the Night" in 1992.

evision comedy teams of all time. Unfortunately, critics didn't like the show, and after two seasons it ended. This was a period when critics seemed to berate anything that reflected anything but urban themes.

In 1991 when he walked on the set of "In the Heat of the Night" to play "Benjamin Sloan" in the episode entitled "An Eye for an Eye," I found him to be so much more than the Lobo character who made me laugh as a child. He was playing a man seeking revenge over the loss of his son to prison. So, he decided to kidnap District Attorney Darnelle's daughter.

He was a star in every sense of the word and could have easily been accorded all that goes along with that after forty years of creating a name known around the world.

After six hours on the job, we would break for lunch and go to catering. It was custom that the actors would go through the line first, followed by the crew. When we arrived at the catering truck and looked up to order our food, there stood Claude in a pressed white apron with a ladle in hand, taking our orders and dishing up our piping hot roast beef with mashed potatoes and gravy.

Instead of going back to his trailer and having the production assistant bring him a plate of food, he stood there serving up meals until the last extra went through the line. Then he filled a plate and joined us at the tables.

As a guest star, actors are only with the show a few days, and most never return. It was a unique experience to find a guest star who went out of his way to be a part of the show family.

Claude served us every day he was on the set. I asked him why he did it. He said that the crew works hard for the actors every day, and it was a way to show them he appreciated what they were doing. I also think it was a wonderful way for Claude to show the crew that he was the same as them. He was simply someone performing his craft to the best of his ability.

I enjoyed the time with Claude, and I had high hopes of working with him again. Alan Autry and I had planned to include him in a project we were developing for television. Unfortunately, Claude passed away before that dream was realized.

Sheriff Lobo Serves Up Some Southern Sense

For an old Georgia boy from just down the road in Nelson, and raised up in Bedford, Indiana, Claude Akins certainly went far. I believe his Southern manners took him a long way — all the way to the top. Once he was there, I believe he never forgot what it was like to be at the bottom. Since many actors begin their careers as waiters, it just shows the great ones are never too good to serve up some food.

And ye have forgotten the exhortation which speaketh unto you as unto children,
My son, despise not thou the chastening of the Lord, nor faint when thou art rebuked of him:
For whom the Lord loveth he chasteneth, and scourgeth every son whom he receiveth.

Hebrews 12:5 & 6

Randall Franks and Mark Johnson — 1992

Dolly Parton

There are few people who can walk through our world and the utterance of one name evokes their image to mind. The name Dolly does that. Dolly Parton worked her way up from meager mountain beginnings to become known on the world stage as a singer, actor, songwriter, and businesswoman. Working with the Herschend family, she gave her name to an amusement park, creating Dollywood and helping create the center of a major tourism center of the Southeast that allows thousands of people the opportunity for work and millions the opportunity of joy and entertainment.

Randall Franks and Dolly Parton backstage at 2010 Awards Show.

© 2010 Randall Franks Media – Karen Peck Gooch

Dolly Parton's work shines to brighten the world.

Her recordings include "I Will Always Love You" and "Here You Come Again." Among her films for the big and little screen are "9 to 5" and "Blue Valley Songbird." After four decades of hit songs and films, she still finds

Encouragers

From left, Sam Bush, Randall Franks, Charlie Bush, youth fiddler, and director Richard Colla on the set of "Blue Valley Songbird."

time through her Dollywood Foundation to support education and improve the quality of life for all children in Sevier County, Tennessee. Begun in Sevier County to provide preschoolers with a book each month from birth until kindergarten, the Foundation's Imagination Library has spread around the world. With the help of local sponsors, the foundation gave away 7.65 million books in 2012.

So what has Dolly done for me in my life? She has never failed to assist me when I called upon her reaching out to help others.
I was honored to work for her in a film production called "Blue Valley Songbird" she fostered along with Freyda Rothstein for Lifetime Cable in 1999. Working for director Richard Colla, my friend Sam Bush and I would bring to life the sounds of a 1970s fiddle contest that her childhood

How many superstars would do this? Dolly Parton straightens Randall Franks's clothes before the two pose for a photo.

208

Dolly Parton

character "Leanna Taylor," played by Teagan Eley, wanted to sing at.

When I came to work in Ringgold at The Catoosa County News, I found myself in the unique situation of having to write about her wedding to Carl Dean in that town. Dolly graciously helped me with the article and even provided their wedding photo.

"We picked Ringgold to get married because for some time in his youth, my husband lived on Missionary Ridge, right on the Tennessee-Georgia border just out-side of Chattanooga," Parton said. "I also liked the idea of 'rings of gold' — Ringgold. I thought that sounded like a good sign."

Dolly Parton

© 2010 Randall Franks Media – Randall Franks

Parton intentionally chose a site away from the mainstream of Nashville.

"I didn't want anybody in Nashville to know that I was getting married because of my business," she said. "So we thought we'd get as far away as we could and still have it as close to Tennessee as we could."

While many couples choose to have a civil ceremony, Parton wanted a church wedding.

"We married in the church as opposed to going to the courthouse. Rev. Don Duvall at the Ringgold Baptist Church married us," Parton said. "But we had to come back on Monday to get married because I refused to get married in the courthouse where we got our license because I wanted to be married in a church."

The wish to be married in a church resulted in two trips to Ringgold for Dolly.

"We went down there, got our license, had to come back home

Encouragers

and then go back," she said. "My mother (Avie Lee Owens Parton) made my little dress, and she was our only witness. So we had to keep my mother over the weekend which was the hardest part. Ha! Just joking."

The couple married Memorial Day, May 30, 1966, and posed for their wedding photo in front of the church.

When I saw her backstage at the Southern Gospel Music Association Awards in the fall of 2010, she shared with me that she was preparing to do yet another film — "Joyful Noise," this time with Queen Latifah. It was to be centered on a choir competition.

We talked about how it would be nice to work together again, and she suggested I get in touch with casting for the film. I had my agent do just that and actually went in to meet with them. It was probably the second most active audition I had ever done as it included singing, dancing, and acting.

While the role was not really what I was hoping for, casting wanted me to come back and see director Todd Graff to do it all over again.

Ultimately, I really was in the groove for those modern group dance numbers, although I gave it my best shot. I was much better the first time around than I was the second, so I did not wind up doing the film.

I found out afterwards that my friend Karen Peck Gooch would lead one of the choruses. It would have been great to work with her as part of her choir.

But the Lord always opens the doors that are meant for you, and I was just glad that Dolly thought enough of me to give me the urging to try to be in the movie.

Maybe we will work together again someday in another movie where I don't have to do modern dance.

Cheese Sticks, a Coke, and a Car Full of Peanuts

As I pulled into the driveway, I wondered if Miss Allie would remember me. It had been a few years since I had seen her, and I was stopping by unannounced. I had been on a long trip that took me by her way.

Folks do not seem to visit like they did years ago.

I thought this might be my last chance to visit with her again, so I walked up to the screen door and knocked. One of her daughters answered and recalled who I was and went to get Miss Allie, so she came and invited me into the sitting room. The house still had the look I remembered — a classic Southern home decorated with what would now be considered antiques but were nearly new when she set up housekeeping. She asked if I would care for something to drink.

Allie Smith
and Randall Franks

She was going to have a Coca-Cola so I joined her. She had the dignity and the air of a Southern belle who had known all the facets of life in the country, but in her advanced years she seemed more comfortable in her Levi blue jeans and plaid work shirt.

Her daughter brought me a Coke in one of those little bottles like you would get for a dime at the barbershop out of one of those machines where the bottles spun around. She also brought a sweet vanilla cake. As we ate, we talked about our families and how the weather had been so hot. As I settled in to the comfortable blue arm chair that I had sat in before, I daydreamed back to my first visit with Miss Allie.

My press agent, Martha Moore, and I walked down South Bond Street, a Victorian residential street of the reconstruction south. It was hot and the smell of roses hung in the air as if one could just reach out and pull one from the sky.

As we walked down the street, folks were gathering on their wide porches to get away from the heat of the day. I could see a small boy

Encouragers

in overalls kicking a can along the sidewalk as a young girl played hopscotch.

I imagined a young Naval Academy cadet walking along with a rose in hand to call on his sweetheart. As we approached the steps that the young cadet would have waited anxiously upon with hat in hand, I looked down at my fiddle case. I wondered if those men in suits on the porch ahead would want to search the case.

The Rosalynn Carter Family Home at 219 South Bond Street in Plains, Georgia.

This quiet southern town was Plains, Georgia. The cadet I imagined was a young Jimmy Carter. The two men on the porch were secret service.

In my life, I had never done anything like this before. I was getting ready to walk in that house and try my first cheese stick.

I bet you thought I was going to say play for the President. Yes, I was going to do that, too. I was going to entertain the whole Carter and Smith clans that had gathered there that day — Chip, Amy, and all.

But for the hostess, the late Allie Murray Smith, mother of Rosalynn Carter, I was there to try her cheese sticks, a favorite of President Carter's.

When the door opened, I was whisked away to the dining room where folks had gathered around a Southern style buffet with all the trimmings, from Southern-fried chicken to freshly prepared potato salad — paprika and all.

President Carter rose to greet me, and then I was once again whisked away to the kitchen where awaited a delight I have not ever known since — the smell of Miss Allie's homemade cheese sticks.

Cheese Sticks, a Coke and a Car Full of Peanuts

© 1994 Randall Franks Media – Martha Moore

Former First Lady Rosalynn and President Jimmy Carter listen as Randall Franks performs a request of "Turkey in the Straw" at a Carter-Smith family gathering in 1994.

(They would make Mickey's mouth water, mouse that is.) I do not know how they were prepared, but I found myself asking for more and more and more. I remember President Carter telling us, "Save some more for me."

After a pleasant visit with the family, we retired to the parlor. As I pulled my fiddle from its case and rosined up the bow, President Carter and I shared stories about pickers that we both know. I began to entertain with a joke or two. Then I pulled my bow across the strings, and time just flew. Amazing Grace, Turkey in the Straw — the tunes went on and on. We sang, we laughed, and we had a time which would make a memory or two.

Jimmy mentioned that he was expecting a call from President Bill Clinton and asked if I would like to play for him as well over the phone. I remember Rosalynn commented how Bill always seemed to be late when he called.

Encouragers

But before the call from the White House came in, duty called for the President and I, and we had to cut the fun short. You see, I was the Grand Marshal of the Plains Day Parade, and we both had our duty to do.

Randall Franks serves as Grand Marshal of the Plains Day Parade in 1994.

© 1994 Randall Franks Media

While we were inside, the town was now brimming with an ocean of onlookers awaiting our cars to go through. After visiting with all the folks, encouraging local youth to live a drug-free life, and sharing a show with attendees, it was time to get on my way and say goodbye to all my friends.

Bobby and Jean Salter of Plain Peanuts and their staff on Main Street were among the city hosts that made my day spectacular. I still stop by to see them when I am by that way.

I had spent the day with one of America's greatest families, and many of those who were part of their lives in Plains.

And though I had worked for peanuts — boiled peanuts, shelled peanuts, unshelled peanuts, salted peanuts, unsalted peanuts, and several types of peanut brittle — a better day I have never known.

My soul melteth for heaviness: strengthen thou me according unto thy word.
Psalm 119:28

Violet Hensley — An Amazing Life

I am honored to have come to know some of the most amazing fiddlers in American history.

Over the past three years, I added to that list someone that when I was a little boy, I saw perform on "The Beverly Hillbillies," and "Captain Kangaroo." That fiddler is America's first woman fiddler of note known to millions through the advent of television and live performances and demonstrations of her craft of making fiddles — Violet Hensley.

On October 21, 2014 she marked her 98th year and throughout that week she greeted fans and friends at the National

Randall Franks and Violet Hensley play a tune at Silver Dollar City in Branson in 2011.

Cowboy and Harvest Festival at Silver Dollar City in Branson, Mo. where she has held court for the past 47 years.

I was privileged to share this occasion with her in a way as many who stopped to see her carried home her autobiography "Whittlin' and Fiddlin' My Own Way: The Violet Hensley Story" which I helped pen.

"I never thought I would be writing about my life, my music and my fiddle makin'," she said. "I could have never dreamed coming from a farm in the backwoods of Arkansas that the things I learned on that farm would make me a TV personality and gain me fame around the world."

The Arkansas Living Treasure Award winner from Yellville,

Encouragers

Violet Hensley appears on "Live! with Regis and Kathie Lee" in 1992.

Arkansas learned to fiddle in 1928 and make fiddles watching her father George W. Brumley in the community of Alamo, Arkansas in 1932.

It was an amazing experience to work with Violet weekly to refine the experiences from her life and compile a book which not only reflects what many rural families endured in America in the 20th century but what was most unique about Violet as she grew artistically, to find folk music stardom at nearly 50.

She raised a family of nine with her late husband Adren while he moved the family from town to town and state to state.

With the advent of the folk music revival, Violet's blossoming musical and fiddle-making talents, caught the attention of Grammy ® winner Jimmy Driftwood and the owners of Silver Dollar City in Branson, Missouri.

She joined the crafter's cast at Silver Dollar City in 1967,

And Judas and Silas, being prophets also themselves, exhorted the brethren with many words, and confirmed them.

Acts 15:32

Violet Hensley — An Amazing Life

becoming part of the City's celebrities who used radio, television, and newspapers to invite visitors to the amusement park.

Sharing her talents in front of millions, Hensley became one of the first woman fiddlers to reach a large international audience appearing at the Smithsonian's Festival of American Folklife, festivals, colleges, and on countless local, regional and national television and radio shows such as "To Tell the Truth" and "Live! with Regis and Kathie Lee"

"I hope folks will enjoy getting a glimpse at what my near century on this world has been," Violet said. "It's been a hoot so far and what's even better is while the book is written — the story continues. I hope folks will join me for what is yet to come, they can start by reading the book."

Her life has inspired me to know that life is lived to encourage others.

Dailey and Vincent perform at the Southern Gospel Music Hall of Fame induction of Don Light in 2009.

Whom I have sent unto you for the same purpose, that ye might know our affairs, and that he might comfort your hearts.

Ephesians 6:22

Moments in Time

We were told there might be moments in life when we entertain angels unaware. Sometimes the person we pause with is not an angel in the biblical sense of one like Gabriel, but the person still acts as God's messenger to us.

Sometimes they manifest simply through a word of encouragement — "I like what you do." Sometimes it's through a new direction or opportunity that the Lord has prepared for us — "Call me next week, I have a project perfect for you;"

Randall Franks with Santa Claus

"Let's get together and do some writing;" or "Could you help me with something?" Sometimes, you are God's instrument for the other person's life, possibly sharing just what they need to hear at that moment to reinforce him or her.

Among these opportunities are moments that grow into something that we could have never envisioned — they are God's moments, His aligning the world, so two of His people might come together and create something wonderful in His plan for their lives that could impact countless others.

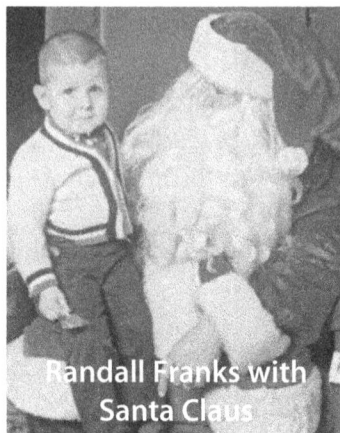

Randall Franks

When we are very young, we usually don't yearn to meet the stars but those who we are taught to honor through the stories that are shared and the media we are encouraged to watch. For instance, the work of Walt Disney was a true influence upon me, both his fantasy and his reflections of life through "The Wonderful World of Disney."

So, as I look back, it does not surprise me that my earliest photos with those outside my family and childhood friends are with Santa Claus and a mouse. While I do not recall them specifically sharing any specific message for my life in the moments we had together, they opened me up for all the encounters ahead. So, the "Moments in Time" you will see within, they were all part of God's plan for me.

A Taste of Giving

Within these pages, you will find a variety of recipes that many friends and celebrities graciously shared in support of my favorite charitable effort. In keeping with their kind donations, a portion of the proceeds of this book will benefit the Share America Foundation, Inc., a Georgia 501C3, that encourages youth in the traditional music and arts of Appalachia. Each year, the program awards the Pearl and Floyd Franks Scholarship to several candidates as they pursue college.

Pearl and Floyd Franks Scholarships recipients include John Rice (fiddle); Deborah Taylor (fiddle); Jarrod Payne (banjo); Jeremy Barker (guitar); Kayla Ray (mandolin); Raven Welch (mandolin); Cody Harvey (banjo); Mike Holloway (bass); Emily Hullender (vocalist); Ryan Stinson (pianist); Tyler Martelli (mandolin); Garrett Arb (banjo); Hunter Moreland (bagpipes); Rachel McConathy (flute); Jonathan Barker (banjo); Westley Harris (fiddle); Wil Markham (fiddle); Aimee Garner (voice); and Emerald Butler (fiddle). Scholarship designees include Kylan Rodgers, 2009; and Nicholas Hickman, 2012. The organization also hosts ten concerts each year at the Ringgold Depot in Ringgold, Georgia, to raise funds for the scholarship and provide opportunities for youth to appear and perform beside seasoned professionals from whom they can learn. Share America Foundation Board members include Randall Franks, president; Gary Knowles, chairman; Jimmy Terrell, vice chairman; James Pelt, secretary; Jerry Robinson, Sr., vice president; and Adam Cathey. For more information about the organization and its programs, write to Share America, P.O. Box 42, Tunnel Hill, GA 30755 or visit shareamericafoundation.org.

Special thanks go to Shirley Smith and the Catoosa Citizens for Literacy for sharing some recipes in this section.

Moments in Time

Randall Franks visits with Australian country singer Wayne Horsburgh at a show in Wisconsin in 1993.

© 1993 Randall Franks Media

© 1993 Randall Franks Media – Donna Tracy

Randall Franks visits with country performer Danny Bell. Bell appeared on Hee Haw and appeared in concert with the Randall Franks Show.

Randall Franks joins Georgia Governor Zell Miller as Miller designates Bluegrass Month in Georgia in 1994. From left are Frank Prince, Franks, Miller, Helen Swanson, and Carl Queen.

Office of the Governor – Phyllis B. Kandul

BBQ Deer

Medium deer roast
1 clove garlic
1 medium onion
1 tsp. liquid smoke
Dash of Tabasco sauce
BBQ sauce
½ tsp. crushed red pepper
Salt and pepper, to taste

Boil roast until tender with garlic and onion. Drain and shred, removing any fat. Add liquid smoke, Tabasco sauce, red pepper, salt and pepper, and barbecue sauce. Preheat oven to 350°. Bake for 15 to 20 minutes covered. Serve with coleslaw.

Jett Williams
Country Music Artist

Jett Williams

Country singer Jett Williams and the Drifting Cowboys entertain audiences around the world. Their work incorporates a blend that includes her original songs from her CD "I'm So Lonesome I Could Cry" and such country classics as "Your Cheatin' Heart" and "Jambalaya" made famous by her late father, country legend Hank Williams. The story of Jett Williams' efforts to prove her real identity as Hank Williams' daughter became the best-selling autobiography "Lost and Found: The Story of Hank Williams' Lost Daughter." Her latest CD is "Honk." Visit www.jettwilliams.com

Moments in Time

Randall Franks and friend Chris Castile in 1994. Castile starred in TV's "Step by Step" and films "Beethoven" and "Beethoven's 2nd."

Fiddlers Art Stamper (1933–2005), Randall Franks and Robert Bowlin share some triple fiddle time for the Grand Ole Opry in 1994.

Randall Franks visits with Johnny Duncan (1938–2006) in 1994. Among the singer's hits were "It Couldn't Have Been Any Better" and "She Can Put Her Shoes Under My Bed Anytime."

Cornbread Salad

(First, make your favorite cornbread.)

1 large can pinto beans
1 can whole kernel corn (drained after cooking)
Cornbread
1 medium onion, diced
1 ½ cups fresh tomatoes, chopped
1 green bell pepper, chopped
Cheese (of your preference)
1 cup sour cream
1 cup mayonnaise
1 package of ranch dressing
Bacon bits and/or croutons

Crumble cornbread into a large bowl. Heat beans and pour over cornbread. Heat corn and pour over for next layer. Chop onions, tomatoes, and green peppers. Add. Add cheese. Combine sour cream, mayonnaise, and ranch dressing. Spread over top. Put bacon bits and/or croutons on top. Chill and stir before serving.

Virginia Davis
mother of Share America Patron Donna Greeson
Ringgold, Georgia

Moments in Time

Randall Franks and singer Leroy Van Dyke in 1994. Among his hits are "Auctioneer" and "Walk on By."

Randall Franks with comedian/actor John Mendoza in 1994, star of the sitcom "The Second Half" and numerous other TV shows and films.

Randall Franks and actor Josh Saviano in 1994. Saviano starred in TV's "The Wonder Years" as well as other films such as "Camp Cucamonga" and "The Wrong Guys."

Summer Squash Casserole

2 lbs. squash
1 cup grated cheddar cheese
2 eggs, beaten
1 tsp. ground sage
1 medium onion, chopped
1 tbsp. sugar
1 tbsp. butter
Salt and pepper, to taste
Paprika for topping, to taste

Cut squash into bite-size pieces and steam for 20 minutes, until tender. Combine all ingredients, except paprika and half of the cheese. Top with paprika and remaining cheese. Bake at 350° for 25 minutes. Bake in 9-inch by 9-inch Pyrex dish, and do not overbake or dish will become dry. Enjoy.

Jeff Carson
Country Music Artist
Submitted by Kim Carson

Jeff Carson

Jeff Carson rode "The Car" to the top of the charts in 1995 and to a win for ACM Video of the Year. As a songwriter, Kenny Rogers recorded his "Until Forever's Gone," a song Carson wrote with Jim Weatherly. Carson's Curb CD, "Real Life," featured the single "Until We Fall Back In Love Again." Carson became a real-life police officer in Franklin, Tennessee, in 2009.

Moments in Time

Randall Franks (center) joins (from left) Sheriff R.V. Chadwell, Sharon Crabtree, Mary Lou Clontz, and Deputy James Hartsock and an audience of Pennington Gap, Virginia, fans in 1994.

Randall Franks joins other surviving members of the Golden River Grass as a pallbearer for folk music entertainer John "Doodle" Thrower of Tallapoosa, Georgia, in 1994.

Randall Franks backstage at the Grand Ole Opry with Roy Clark. Among the Hee Haw star's hits are "Yesterday," "Thank God and Greyhound" and "Under the Double Eagle."

'Nothing Else Like It' Meat Loaf

Roy Clark

1 lb. ground beef
1 lb. ground Italian sausage
1/3 cup chopped onion
1/3 cup chopped green pepper
12 oz. can diced tomatoes
1 whole egg
1/3 cup bread crumbs
1 tbsp. Italian seasoning

Combine all ingredients in large bowl and mix well using clean hands. Divide and shape into two loaves. Place in 9-inch by 13-inch pan. Bake at 350° for 1 hour covered, 15 minutes uncovered. While you're at it, throw a couple of baking potatoes in the oven at the same time! Enjoy!

Roy Clark
Country Music Artist

The actor, comedian, and legendary guitarist and banjo player hosted Hee Haw for over twenty years. As an actor, he appeared in movies and on shows such as The Beverly Hillbillies. The Country Music Hall of Fame® member won a Grammy for his recording of the "Alabama Jubilee" and enjoyed numerous charts songs. The two-time Entertainer of the Year has appeared in some of the world's biggest venues and is a member of the Grand Ole Opry. Visit www.royclark.org

Moments in Time

Randall Franks guest stars on TV's "Reno's Old Time Music Festival" backed by Jim and Jesse and the Virginia Boys in 1994.

Randall Franks backstage at the Grand Ole Opry with Billy Walker. Among his hits were "Funny How Time Slips Away," "Cross the Brazos at Waco," and "Charlie's Shoes."

Randall Franks with actor Grant Aleksander during his run on "All My Children" as Alec McIntyre." He starred in several soap operas including "The Guiding Light."

7 Layer Dip

16 oz. can refried beans
1 package taco seasoning
1 can bean dip
6-8 tomatoes
3 avocadoes (optional)
5 scallions
8 oz. sour cream
1 cup pitted olives
2 tbsp. lemon juice
1 lb. sharp shredded cheese
½ cup mayonnaise

Mix refried beans and bean dip. Spread into a casserole dish. Mix avocadoes, mayo, and lemon juice and spread over bean mixture. Mix sour cream and taco seasoning and spread over previous layer. Dice and sprinkle tomatoes, then scallions, and then sliced olives. Sprinkle with cheese. Cover overnight in refrigerator. Serve with tortilla chips.

Nan Pinkston, Share America Patron
Ringgold, Georgia

Moments in Time

Charlie Daniels plays guitar as Randall Franks fiddles and they lead a host of stars for a song during a special media event in Wichita, Kansas.

Randall Franks and Charlie Daniels backstage at a 1995 Wichita, Kansas concert. Among his hits are "The Devil Went Down to Georgia" and "The South's Gonna Do It Again."

Randall Franks regularly stopped by to interview with Ann Varnum (left) at WTVY in Dothan, Alabama. This visit was in 1995, and they join Mr. Bruce and Teresa Smith on the set.

230

Banana Bread

1 cup sugar
2 cups plain flour, unsifted
½ cup margarine
3 tbsp. sour cream
2 eggs, separated
1 tsp. soda
½ tsp. salt
4 ripe bananas
1 tsp. vanilla flavoring

Cream margarine. Add egg yolks and sugar. Add flour, salt, soda, sour cream, and bananas. Beat egg whites, fold into mixture. Add vanilla flavoring. Pour into greased loaf pan. Cook at 350° for 1 hour or until done.

Ann Nix
Former Share America Task Force Member

Moments in Time

Randall Franks shared the stage with these two Grand Ole Opry legends, Jan Howard and Jeannie Seely, for the Ernest Tubb Record Shop in 1995.

© 1995 Randall Franks Media

© 1995 Randall Franks Media

Randall Franks and The Moffatts visit at Fan Fair 1995. Their music was country at this point, but they went on to become one of the biggest pop/rock acts at the turn of the millenium.

Randall Franks and Grandpa Jones (1913–2008) pause backstage in Nashville in 1995. Among his hits are "8 More Miles to Louisville," "Rattler," and "Mountain Dew."

© 1995 Randall Franks Media

232

Don't Touch My Butterscotch Pie

Jeannie Seely

1 cup brown sugar
¼ cup cornstarch
½ tsp. salt
Mix in saucepan and gradually stir in:
1 cup water
1 2/3 cup milk
1/3 cup butter
3 egg yolks
1 ½ tsp. vanilla
Meringue (recipe not included)

Grand Ole Opry star Jeannie Seely helped to reshape the role of women in country music through a strong determination to turn her dreams into a reality. Through her dedication to her craft, in 1966 she won a GRAMMY® for "Don't Touch Me." She penned the number one song "Leavin' and Sayin' Goodbye" for Faron Young in 1972. After thirteen consecutive years with songs on the charts, she continues to thrill audiences with new recordings, films, videos, and live performances and appearances in stage plays such as Always, Patsy Cline. She also adds nominations and awards to her long list of accomplishments. Visit www.jeannieseely.com.

Mix brown sugar, cornstarch, and salt in saucepan. Gradually stir in water, milk, and butter. Cook over medium heat, stirring constantly, until mixture thickens and boils. Boil 1 minute. Remove from heat and stir some of hot mixture into 3 egg yolks, slightly beaten. Then blend into the hot mixture in pan. Boil 1 more minute, stirring constantly. Remove from heat and blend in vanilla. Pour into baked pie shell. Top with meringue and bake 8 to 10 minutes at 400° until lightly browned.

Jeannie Seely, Country Music Artist

Moments in Time

Randall Franks and Vern Gosdin (1934–2009) visit at Fan Fair in 1995. Among Gosdin's hits were "Chiseled in Stone," "Way Down Deep," and "Do You Believe Me Now."

Randall Franks and Grand Ole Opry star Stonewall Jackson share the stage for the Ernest Tubb Record Shop in 1995.

Randall Franks and Johnny Lee appear in California at ACM Fan Fest in 1995. Among his hits were "Lookin' for Love," "The Yellow Rose," and "You Could Have Heard a Heart Break."

Mexican Lasagna

Annette O' Toole

As "Martha Kent" on Smallville, Annette O'Toole spends a lot of her time teaching her son, a young Superman played by Tom Welling, how to deal with his superpowers. In her own 2000 series The Huntress, she taught the bad guys a thing or two as bounty huntress Dottie Thorson. Acting since childhood, O'Toole's career included time on Gunsmoke. She has been a presence on television and in film for four decades.

1 ½ lbs. ground turkey
1 oz. package taco seasoning mix
15 oz. can diced tomatoes
2 8-oz. cans tomato sauce
4 oz. can diced green chilies
1 small container ricotta cheese
2 eggs, beaten
10 corn tortillas
1 lb. shredded Jack cheese

Cook ground turkey in large skillet over medium heat until browned and cooked through. Drain off fat, if any. Add taco seasoning mix, tomatoes, tomato sauce, and chilies. Mix well and bring to boil. Reduce heat and simmer uncovered 10 minutes. Combine ricotta cheese and eggs in a small bowl. Spread half of the turkey mixture in 9-inch by 13-inch baking dish. Place five tortillas over the turkey mixture. Spread half the ricotta cheese mixture over the tortillas and sprinkle with half the shredded jack cheese. Repeat layers. Bake uncovered at 350° until cheese is melted and lightly browned for 20 to 30 minutes. Let stand 10 minutes before cutting into squares for serving. Makes 6 to 8 servings.

Annette O'Toole, Actress

Moments in Time

Randall Franks entertains a young fan at ACM Fan Fest in Pomona, California, in 1995.

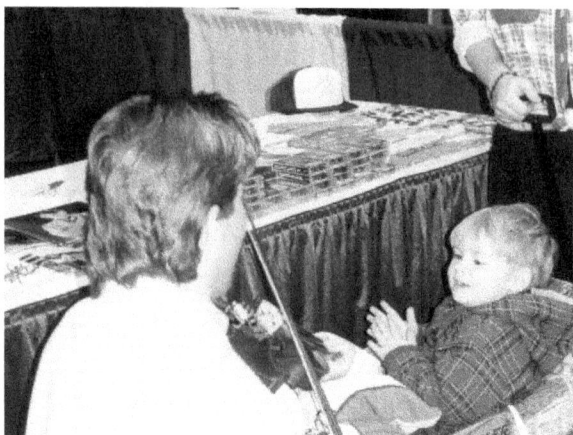

© 1995 Randall Franks Media – Vada Nance

© 1995 Randall Franks Media

Randall Franks and Tanya Tucker were Fan Fair neighbors exhibiting side by side as they visited thousands of fans. Among her hits were "Delta Dawn" and "I Won't Take Less Than Your Love."

Randall Franks and Dan Seals (1948–2009) back-stage after entertaining a large crowd in Saltville, Virginia. His hits included "Meet Me in Montana," "Bop," and "You Still Move Me."

© 1995 Randall Franks Media

Pineapple/Cheese Casserole

20 oz. can pineapple chunks in juice
½ cup sugar
3 tbsp. flour
1 cup sharp cheddar cheese, grated
¼ cup butter or margarine melted
½ cup Ritz cracker crumbs

Drain pineapple, reserving 3 tablespoons of liquid. Combine sugar and flour. Stir in pineapple juice. Add cheese and pineapple. Mix well. Spoon into one-quart greased casserole dish. Combine melted butter and cracker crumbs. Sprinkle over top of pineapple mixture. Bake at 350° for 20 to 30 minutes until lightly browned.

Jo Walker-Meador
Country Music Hall of Fame Member
Country Music Association
Executive Director 1962-1991

Moments in Time

Randall Franks and actor/musician Branscombe Richmond. He was Bobby Sixkiller on the hit television series Renegade in 1995. He has starred in numerous films and TV shows.

Randall Franks visits with country artist Chely Wright at Fan Fair 1995. Among her hits were "Single White Female" and "Shut Up and Drive."

Randall Franks and singer/actor Gary Morris visit at a Music City News event in 1995. He starred on Broadway in "Les Misérables" and made "Wings Beneath My Wings" a hit.

Grilled Veggies ala Richmond

Eggplant
Red and green peppers
Broccoli
Asparagus
Squash (whatever is in season)
(Check out your local veggie stand and see what
appeals to you. Most veggies that are solid and not
leafy will work.)

Cut vegetables into chunks/slices about 4 inches by 4 inches. For the asparagus, the trick is to bend the rough end until it breaks naturally. That way you have just the most edible part of the stalk. Pour enough high grade virgin olive oil over the vegetables and make sure that they are well covered in oil. Let them marinate for a half hour. Cook them over medium to hot coals until they are al dente or you can put a fork in them fairly easily. Do not overcook because they will get soggy. Eat right away. These are also good for leftovers the next day. They are easy to microwave and have with your leftover meats.
In our house, the most favorite meals are the ones we cook out on the grill. With all the health notices on eating too much meat, we've found that most of our favorite vegetables grill spectacularly. Because we live in California, we can grill year-round. The secret is that olive oil is known to be one of the best oils for your health, and it seems to bring out the natural flavors in the veggies for a lip-smackin' meal.
Branscombe Richmond, Actor/Music Artist

Moments in Time

Randall and Western Flyer Danny Myrick, Chris Marion, T. J. Klay, Bruce Gust, Steve Charles, and Roger Helton at Fan Fair 1995. Among their hits was "What Will You Do with M-E?"

Randall Franks hosts the SPBGMA Bluegrass Music Awards in Nashville in 1995 — trying to take home as many awards as he could carry.

Randall Franks visits with gospel promoter Leslie Chastain and gospel singer Scott Thomas during a 1995 songwriting session.

Crazy Crust Apple Pie

1 cup all purpose flour
1 tsp. baking soda
½ tsp. salt
1/3 cup sugar
1 egg
2/3 cup shortening or oil
¾ cup water
1 lb. can apple pie filling
1 tbsp. lemon juice
½ tsp. apple pie spice or cinnamon

In a small mixing bowl, combine flour, baking powder, salt, sugar, egg, oil, and water. Blend well. Beat for 2 minutes at medium mixer speed. Pour batter into a 9-inch by 1 ¼-inch pie pan. Combine apples, lemon juice, and spice. Pour into center of batter. Do not stir. Bake at 425° for 45 to 50 minutes. The pie makes its own crust. If using fresh apples, combine these ingredients to create the filling:

2 ¼ cups peeled sliced apples
1 tbsp. lemon juice
1/3 cup sugar
2 tbsp. flour
½ tsp. spice or cinnamon

Bessie Yarbray

Moments in Time

Randall Franks with mother-daughter beauty queens — both Mrs. Alabama. Franks sang a song to them live on television.

Randall Franks and country singer Marty Stuart visit backstage in 1995 at a Dalton, Georgia, concert. Stuart entertains on "The Marty Stuart Show" on RFD-TV.

Gene Watson and Randall Franks visit backstage in 1995. Among his hits are "Farewell Party," "Paper Rosie," and "Fourteen Carat Mind."

Hearty Chicken Pot Pie

10 ¾ oz. can condensed chicken broth
1 1/3 cup water, divided
1 ½ cups thinly sliced carrots (4 medium)
1 ½ cups red potatoes, scrubbed and diced (3 medium)
2 tbsp. olive oil
2 cups quartered medium mushrooms
1 medium onion, coarsely chopped
1 cup frozen peas
1/3 cup all-purpose flour
9-inch unbaked refrigerated pie crust
2 ½ cups chopped cooked chicken

Combine broth, one cup of water, carrots, and potatoes in a medium saucepan. Bring to a boil; reduce heat and simmer over low heat for 10 minutes. Preheat oven to 425°. Heat oil in large skillet over medium heat. Add mushrooms and onions; sauté until softened for about 5 minutes. Stir in broth mixture and peas. Whisk remaining 1/3 cup of water into flour until smooth. Whisk into vegetable mixture. Increase heat to medium-high and bring to a boil. Spread out pie crust on floured surface. Measure and roll if necessary to fit one inch larger than top of two-quart shallow baking dish. Stir chicken into vegetable mixture and transfer into baking dish. Place crust over filling. Trim and flute edge. Cut a scalloped round from center. Bake until golden brown.

Leola Craig
Actress

Moments in Time

Randall Franks and Johnny Counterfit share the stage in Nashville, Tennessee, in 1995. The award winning comedian is one of the most versatile impressionists in the business.

© 1995 Randall Franks Media

© 1995 Randall Franks Media

Three country stars sonic in style in their limousine — Giant star Chris Ward, Liberty star Noah Gordon and Crimson star Randall Franks in 1995.

Randall Franks serves as musical consultant as Alan Autry films "Hubba Bubba" for TNT. The commercial would promo "In the Heat of the Night" coming to the cable network in 1996.

© 1995 Randall Franks Media

Grandma Hazel's Strawberry Cake

1 box white cake mix
1 small package strawberry Jell-O
2/3 cup oil
¼ cup water
4 eggs
½ cup frozen strawberries including the juice (thawed)

Combine cake mix, Jell-O, cooking oil, and water. Beat well. Add eggs, one at a time, and beat well after each addition. Add strawberries and beat well. Pour into three layer pans. Bake at 300° until done.

Icing
1 box powdered sugar
1 teaspoon vanilla
1 stick margarine
½ cup strawberries drained

Cream together sugar, vanilla, and margarine. Add strawberries. Mix well, but don't let icing get too soft. Spread over cake.

My Grandma Hazel Ferguson used to make this cake for me as a child on up until I was grown and she passed away. I loved it then, and every time I bake it now I think of her. It's never as good as hers, but it's always great! She had that extra ingredient of a Grandma's love that she put into it.

Larry Ferguson, Music Producer and Manager

Moments in Time

Randall Franks pauses with fellow Blue Grass Boys Dana Cupp and Tater Tate (1931–2007) at a Grand Ole Opry appearance in 1996.

Randall Franks and country singer Noah Gordon wrote songs together in the 1990s. Here they are visiting at Fan Fair 1996. Among his hits were "The Blue Pages" and "I Need a Break."

Randall Franks and banjo great J.D. Crowe visit at an Opry performance in 1996. Crowe is a multi award-winning banjo stylist and band leader.

Shrimp Newbourg

1 lb. medium shrimp
2 quarts water
Salt and pepper flakes
½ cup vinegar
4 tbsp. flour
4 tbsp. butter
2 cups milk
¼ cup white wine
2 tbsp. lemon juice
Salt and pepper

Bring water to a boil, add vinegar and salt and pepper flakes. Add shrimp. Cook for 3 to 4 minutes. Drain. Peel shrimp, set aside.
Melt butter, add flour, and simmer about 3 minutes. Add milk, and stir constantly until creamy and bubbly. Add wine, lemon, salt, and pepper while hot. Add shrimp. Heat thoroughly.

Cristy Lane
Country and Gospel Music Artist

Moments in Time

Randall Franks and Ricky Skaggs take a moment at a Grand Ole Opry show in 1996. From his 1981 "Waitin' for the Sun to Shine" to 2013 "Cluck Ol' Hen," fourteen Grammys did he win.

© 1996 Randall Franks Media – Donna Tracy

© 1996 Randall Franks Media – Donna Tracy

Randall Franks visits with Sophie Tipton and Louise Tomberlain at the Carl Tipton Memorial Bluegrass Festival in Leanna, Tennessee, in 1996.

Randall Franks and actress Kaitlin Cullum take a musical break on the set of "Grace Under Fire" in Los Angeles in 1996. Among her projects were "Galaxy Quest," and "8 Simple Rules."

© 1996 Randall Franks Media

Banana Nut Bread

½ cup butter
1 ½ cup sugar
3 eggs
1 ½ cups sour cream
2 tsp. soda
1 tsp. vanilla
4-5 bananas, mashed
½ teaspoon salt
2 ½ cups all purpose flour
1 cup chopped pecans

Cream butter, sugar, and eggs together. Add mashed bananas and vanilla and mix well.

In a separate bowl, mix sour cream and soda together and let stand until foamy.

Mix dry ingredients in a large bowl. Then add the other mixtures and mix well. (You may add the pecans at this point if desired.)

Pour into two greased and floured 9-inch by 5-inch loaf pans and bake 50 minutes at 350° or until a toothpick inserted comes out clean.

Let cool slightly before taking up. (I will let one cool completely, wrap well, and freeze for another time.)

Sharon White Skaggs
The Whites
Country Music Artists

Moments in Time

Randall Franks is backstage with Jeannie C. Riley and a young fan, her grandson, at a performance for the Ernest Tubb Record Shop in 1996. Among her hits was "Harper Valley P.T.A."

Randall Franks visits backstage with Grand Ole Opry star Stonewall Jackson at a performance for the Ernest Tubb Record Shop in 1996.

Randall Franks visits with actor Michael Martin. The duo would share the screen in the 1997 film "Phoenix Falling" with Martin playing the nemesis to Franks.

Hawaii Banana Nut Bread

3 cups plain flour
1 tsp. soda
1 tsp. salt
1 tsp. cinnamon
1 cup nuts, (I use English walnuts)
3 eggs, beaten
1 ½ cup oil
8 oz. can crushed pineapple
2 cups sugar
2 tsp. vanilla
2 cups mashed bananas

Preheat oven to 350°. Mix together flour, soda, salt, cinnamon, and nuts. Set aside. In separate bowl, beat together eggs, oil, pineapple, sugar, vanilla, and bananas. Stir in dry ingredients until moist. Makes one bundt pan or three coffee can size. Bake 50 to 60 minutes, or line five mini loaf pans (2-inch by 5-inch by 3-inch) with wax paper and bake 45 minutes in 350° oven.

Stonewall Jackson
Country Music Artist

Stonewall Jackson

Grand Ole Opry star Stonewall Jackson, who grew up in South Georgia, has performed as part of the famed show since 1956. With around 40 hits to his credit including his career song "Waterloo" he has developed a legion of fans who love his straight-forward country sound. Other famous songs include "Don't Be Angry," "B.J. the D.J.,"and "I Washed My Hands in Muddy Water." He received the Ernest Tubb Memorial Award in 1997.

Moments in Time

Randall Franks joins actors Haley Joel Osment and Kathryn Zaremba on the set of "Foxworthy" for some musical mirth in 1996. Osment is an Academy Award nominee.

© 1996 Randall Franks Media

© 1996 Randall Franks Media

Randall Franks and Australian cowboy star Smokey Dawson (1913–2008) smile in 1996. Dawson was a favorite of Australians through his radio shows, music, and comic books.

From left, Randall Franks, Anthony Bailey, David Davis, and Tom Ewing share the stage at Country's Barbeque in Columbus, Georgia, in 1996.

© 1996 Randall Franks Media

Maple Cranberry Sauce

12 oz. fresh cranberries (1 bag), well rinsed
1 cup maple syrup
1 cup raspberry-cranberry juice
Grated zest of 1 orange
1 cup walnut halves

Combine cranberries, maple syrup, juice, and zest in a saucepan. Bring to a boil, then lower heat to medium and cook until the cranberries pop open, about 10 minutes.

Skim off any foam that has formed on the surface of the mixture, and stir in the walnuts. Allow to cool, then cover and refrigerate. Sauce will keep for 3 to 4 days.

Tom Ewing
Former member of Bill Monroe's Blue Grass Boys and Jim and Jesse's Virginia Boys

Moments in Time

Randall Franks appears on stage at a star-studded evening of country music in Nashville, Tennessee, in March 1997.

Actor Tommy Barnes played a bad guy in two Randall Franks films, "Phoenix Falling" and "Firebase Nine." Among his other projects were "The Green Mile" and "Social Path."

Randall Franks pauses on the set with director Eric Straton, producer Ruthanna Straton, and the cast of "Phoenix Falling."

'Speck' Hearon's Holiday Broccoli Casserole

1 package frozen broccoli, or about 2 cups fresh
1 can cream of mushroom soup
1 cup mayonnaise
½ to ¾ cup finely grated sharp cheddar
A little grated onion (1/8 to ¼ cup)
Dash of worcestershire
Salt and pepper
6 eggs
Bread or cracker crumbs (optional)

Cook broccoli until tender in salted water. Drain and mash or chop finely. Add soup, mayonnaise, cheese, onion, and seasonings. Fold in beaten eggs. Pour into 2-quart casserole dish and top with crumbs if desired. (You don't have to grease the casserole, but I usually spray on a little Pam and spread it around.) Bake at 300° for 1 to 1 ½ hours, until top begins to turn golden. Best to test center with straw for doneness if not sure. Casserole will rise when baking, then fall a bit when out of oven.
Asparagus may be substituted for broccoli.
This makes a great holiday dinner dish.

Martha and Eddie Adcock
Bluegrass Music Artists

Moments in Time

Randall Franks and singer/songwriter Dorata Roberts visit at Fan Fair 1997.

© 1997 Randall Franks Media

© 1997 Randall Franks Media – Donna Tracy

Randall Franks and the Hagars — Jim (1941-2008) and Jon (1941-2009) — appear in concert in 1997. The Hagars starred on Hee Haw and acted in several TV productions in twin roles.

Randall Franks and Janie Fricke visit at a Music City News event in 1997. Among Fricke's hits were "He's a Heartache," Your Heart Is Not in It," and "Always Have, Always Will."

© 1997 Randall Franks Media

Pecan Cheesecake Pie

½ (15 oz.) package refrigerated pie crusts
1 cup semisweet chocolate morsels
3 tbsp. whipping cream
8 oz. package cream cheese, softened
4 large eggs
¾ cup sugar divided

2 tsp. vanilla extract, divided
¼ tsp. salt
1 cup light corn syrup
3 tbsp. butter or margarine, melted
1 ½ cups pecan halves
Chocolate syrup (optional)

Preheat oven to 350°. Unroll pie crust, fit into a 9-inch pie pan. Fold edges under and crimp. Microwave chocolate morsels and whipping cream in a small glass bowl at medium (50 percent power) 1 to 1 ½ minutes or until morsels begin to melt. Whisk until smooth. Set aside. Beat cream cheese, one egg, ½ cup sugar, 1 tsp. vanilla, and salt at medium speed with an electric mixer until smooth. Pour chocolate mixture into pie crust, spreading evenly. Pour cream cheese mixture over chocolate layer. Whisk together corn syrup, melted butter, remaining three eggs, remaining ¾ cup sugar, and remaining 1 tsp. vanilla. Stir in pecans; pour over cream cheese layer. Bake at 350° for 55 minutes or until set, shielding pie after about 45 minutes. Cool completely on wire wrack. Drizzle each slice with chocolate syrup if desired.

Jill Clark, Share America Task Force Member
Ringgold, Georgia

Moments in Time

Randall Franks starred as "Captain Morgan Fairhope" in the 1997 film "Firebase Nine." Fairhope is an army doctor sent to a forward fire-base in the Vietnam War.

Randall Franks appears in concert with Blackhawk — Van Stephens, Dave Robbins, and Henry Paul. Among their hits were "Goodbye Says It All," and "I'm Not Strong Enough to Say No."

Randall Franks and actor Michael Martin go over some stunts for a fight scene for the film "Firebase Nine" in 1997.

Cream Cheese Cake

3 8-oz. packages of cream cheese
1 pint sour cream
4 eggs
1 ½ cups sugar
½ tsp. vanilla

Mix cream cheese and eggs with wooden spoon — when softened use a mixer. Add sugar, vanilla and sour cream. Continue to mix until very smooth. Grease 10-inch spring pan well, side and all. Pour mixture into pan. Place into another pan filled with ½ inch of water. Bake at 350° for 1 hour and 10 minutes. After 1 hour and 10 minutes, turn the oven off and leave the cake in warm oven for 30 minutes more. Remove and cool completely.

Dot Curley

Moments in Time

Randall Franks and pop/country singer Sylvia (Hutton) appear in concert in 1997. Among her hits were "Nobody," "Fallin' in Love," and "I Love You By Heart."

Randall Franks's country sounds were aided by this group of talented musicians led by Grammy winning producer/musician Randy Kohrs (third from left) in 1997.

Randall Franks hosts a historic concert in 1997 at the Ryman Auditorium. The concert included Highway 101, Kentucky Headhunters, Rhett Akins, and Ronna Reeves.

Cat Island Whoo Doggies

1 package of smokey links (Nathan's or Hebrew National hot dogs may be substituted, but it will not be as good as smokey links)
1 lb. of sliced bacon (good stuff)
Thick sliced cheddar (American cheese can be substituted if kids insist)

Cook smokey links or hot dogs in water per package instructions. Slice cooked links lengthwise, starting ¼ inch in from each end and only cut to half depth, creating a pocket. Fold over cheddar and stuff/overstuff into link pocket. Wrap a piece of bacon around each smokey link. Secure bacon with a toothpick on each end. Broil (using top broiler only) on mid level shelf until the bacon is lightly cooked and cheese melted. Serve with catsup (remove toothpicks prior to giving to children). Whoo Doggies are typically served without a bun but with potato chips on the side.

David Lee Murphy

With thirteen chart songs, including "Loco" and the number one "Dust on the Bottle," country artist David Lee Murphy marks twenty years in 2014 since his MCA Nashville debut. His music has appeared in film soundtracks, including "8 Seconds" and "Black Dog." He is also a songwriter who has helped create hits for other country singers. His work includes Jason Aldean's "Big Green Tractor," Kenny Chesney's "Living in Fast Forward," and Thompson Square's "Are You Gonna Kiss Me or Not." For more information, visit www.davidlee.com or www.myspace.com/davidleemurphy.

David Lee Murphy, Country Music Artist

Moments in Time

After twenty years apart, Peachtree Pickers — Randall Franks, (from left) Greg Earnest, Mark Nelson, and Greg Rogers performed a special show for the WRFG Peach Blossom Festival.

Randall Franks performs as part of "Doc" Scott's Last Real Old Time Medicine Show at the Georgia Music Hall of Fame in 1998 with Harry Mullins and "Doc" Tommy Scott.

Randall Franks with Heat fan/country singer Terri Clark at Music City News event in 1998.
Among her hits were "If I Were You," "Poor, Poor Pitiful Me," and "Girls Lie Too."

Boiled Chocolate Oatmeal Cookies

2 cups sugar
¼ cup cocoa
½ cup milk
1 stick margarine
2 ½ cups minute oatmeal (uncooked — not instant)
½ cup peanut butter
2 tsp. vanilla

Combine sugar and cocoa in saucepan. Add margarine and milk. Bring to boil on medium heat. When it reaches a rolling boil, set timer for 3 minutes and cook. Then remove from heat and add vanilla; stir in peanut butter, then stir in oatmeal. Quickly drop by tablespoons on wax paper. Must work fast. Makes about 3 dozen, depending on size dropped.

Sandra Scott Whitworth
Ramblin' Tommy Scott Show

Moments in Time

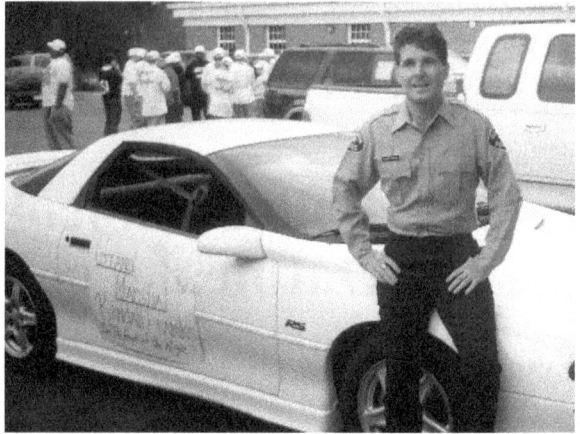

Randall Franks grand marshals the Wedowee, Alabama, Christmas Parade in 1998.

Randall Franks and singer Dwight Whitley share some time at Fan Fair 1998. A musical influence on his younger brother Keith, his most popular recording is "Brotherly Love."

Randall Franks and Gilbert Hancock perform at the American Legion Hall in Zephyrhills, Florida, on March 14, 1998.

Mayonnaise Cake

2 cups flour
4 tsp. baking cocoa
1 cup mayonnaise
1 cup warm water
1 tsp. baking soda
1 cup sugar
Confectioner's sugar

Mix flour, sugar, and cocoa. Add baking soda, mayonnaise and water. Bake for 25 to 40 minutes at 325° in a greased bundt pan. When a toothpick, after insertion, comes out of cake clean, it is done. Sprinkle with confectioner's sugar.

Kathy Porter
Covington, Georgia

Moments in Time

Randall Franks and Aaron Tippin had side by side booths at Fan Fair 1999. Among his hits were "There Ain't Nothing Wrong with the Radio" and "You've Got to Stand For Something."

Randall Franks joins the Wildwood Girls — Sue Koskela and Kim Koskela — on a horseback performance of "Happy Trails" in the Opryland Hotel in 1999.

Randall Franks joins baseball player Rick Wilkins to raise charity funds in Florida at the Rick Wilkins Golf Tournament in 1999.

Turkey Dressing

2 tbsp. vegetable shortening
2 cups self-rising cornmeal
1 ¾ cups buttermilk
½ loaf (10 slices) white bread
2 large onions, chopped
2 ribs celery, chopped

1 stick (½ cup) butter
6 eggs
3 tbsp. dried sage or 2 tbsp. powdered sage
1 tbsp. cider vinegar
1 tsp. salt
1 tsp. pepper
Turkey broth

Preheat oven to 450°. In a 10-inch iron skillet, heat shortening until almost smoking. Combine cornmeal and buttermilk. Mix well and pour into a small skillet. Bake for 20 minutes or until golden brown. Cool. Crumble into a large bowl. Toast white bread slices, cut into squares, and mix with cornbread. In a skillet, sauté onions and celery in butter until tender. Add to cornbread mixture. Boil 3 of the eggs until hard cooked; cool and chop. Add boiled eggs and remaining 3 eggs to cornbread mixture. Add sage, vinegar, salt, and pepper. Mix well. Add turkey broth to make the mixture the consistency of cake batter. Pour into a greased and floured pan. Bake at 350° for 45 minutes. Makes 10 to 12 servings.

Pat White's Recipe
Sharon White Skaggs, The Whites
Country Music Artist

Moments in Time

Randall Franks and comedian Ralph Harris shared the stage for a show in Ponte Vedra, Florida, in 1999.

© 1999 Randall Franks Media

© 1999 Randall Franks Media

Randall Franks and Sam Bush (left) appeared for director Richard Colla (right) in Dolly Parton's "Blue Valley Songbird" in 1999. Charlie Bush and the young fiddler were extras.

Randall Franks was on the road with his Hollywood Hillbilly Jamboree. From left, Gary Waldrep, Bill Everett, Franks, Roger Hammock, and Ryan Robertson were the band.

© 1999 Randall Franks Media

Any Flavor Lush

First Layer:
1 cup flour
1 stick margarine
½ cup pecans or sliced almonds

Second Layer:
1 cup powdered sugar
8-oz. package of cream cheese
1 cup Cool Whip (from 9 oz. container)

Third Layer:
2 packages Jell-O ® instant pudding (any flavor)
3 cups milk

First Layer: Mix like pie dough and press into bottom of an 11-inch by 7-inch pan. Bake at 375° for 15 minutes. Let cool slightly.
Second Layer: Mix ingredients and spread on first layer.
Third Layer: Mix pudding with milk. Pour over second layer. Top with remaining Cool Whip.

Note: Lemon, vanilla, and coconut pudding are good in this recipe.

Jean and Robert Reedy, Share America Patrons Harrisonburg, Virginia

Moments in Time

Randall Franks visits with the Heaters Club, a group of dedicated fans of "In the Heat of the Night," in Covington, Georgia, in 1999.

Randall Franks snapped this shot of bluegrass star David Davis in Mt. Wolf, Pennsylvania, when they performed in concert together in 1999.

Randall Franks directs a group of youth in a skit at Whole Life Ministries in Augusta, Georgia, in 1999.

Cheesy Chicken-Broccoli Rollups

6 thinly sliced chicken breast fillets
2 tbsp. olive oil
½ cup shredded sharp cheddar cheese
½ cup shredded mozzarella cheese
1 cup cooked chopped broccoli
1 tbsp. finely chopped onions
1 can cream of chicken soup or cream of chicken and mushroom soup
½ cup sour cream
1 tbsp. butter
Cherry tomatoes
Parsley sprigs

Lightly brown chicken breasts in olive oil about 1 minute on each side.
Cook broccoli and drain well. While still warm, mix in the cheeses, onion, and butter. In a small bowl, combine and mix well soup and sour cream.
Place chicken in a lightly greased shallow baking pan. Spoon broccoli mixture on top of each piece tightly and pour soup-sour cream mixture over top. Bake uncovered at 350° for 25 minutes. Garnish with cherry tomatoes and parsley sprigs.

Ann Reeves
Calhoun, Georgia

Moments in Time

Doodle Thrower is honored in Tallapoosa, Georgia. From left are his band and widow, C.J. and Wesley Clackum, Ezell Thrower, Gene Daniell, James Watson, and Randall Franks.

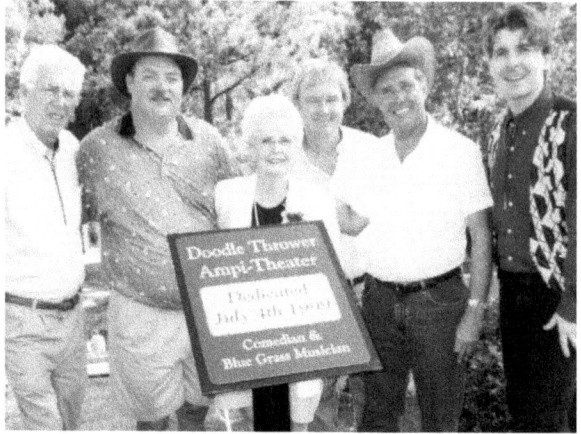

© 1999 Randall Franks Media

© 1999 Randall Franks Media – Mary Miller

Randall Franks and his Hollywood Hillbilly Jamboree performs in Swainsboro, Georgia, in 1999.

Randall Franks in uniform again in 2000, this time as a security guard for Faith Hill in a commercial for Alltel Communications.

© 2000 Randall Franks Media

Great Meat Loaf

1 ½ to 2 lbs. hamburger meat (or ground turkey)
1 can tomato sauce (reserve ½ can)
1 package McCormick meat loaf seasoning
1 egg
Bread crumbs

Mix all ingredients together. Bake 1 to 1 ½ hours at 350° or until done. Note: Reserve half the can of tomato sauce to pour on top of meatloaf before baking.

Faith Hill
Country Music Artist

Faith Hill

Five-time Grammy winner Faith Hill has sold more than 30 million records and has had thirteen number one singles, twenty number one videos and more than twenty music industry awards. Her latest releases include The Hits (2007) and Joy to the World. Visit www.faithhill.com.

Moments in Time

Randall Franks and Grammy nominee Ty Herndon visited fans side by side at Fan Fair 2000. Among his hits were "Livin' in a Moment," "It Must Be Love," and "What Mattered Most."

Randall Franks at the Nashville premiere of Dolly Parton's "Blue Valley Songbird." Franks played a 1970s twin fiddler in the movie with Sam Bush.

Randall Franks and Daryle Singletary visit at Fan Fair in 2000. Among his hits were "I Let Her Lie," "Amen Kind of Love," and "Too Much Fun."

ET's Texas Troubadour Chili

2 lbs. ground beef
1 cup water
½ cup shortening or lard
½ cup chopped onions
2 tbsp. minced garlic
4 tbsp. chili powder
2 tbsp. paprika
½ tsp. cayenne pepper
1 tsp. salt
Juice of 1 lemon
3 oz. tomato sauce

Cook beef in a pot of cold water until it boils and meat is brown. Skim off excess grease. In a small skillet, combine enough flour and one cup water to make a thin paste. Cook until browned. Add to beef. Add remaining ingredients and cook slowly for 1 hour. Makes 6 to 8 servings.

David McCormick of Ernest Tubb Record Shops
The Late Ernest Tubb — Country Music Artist

Ernest Tubb

The late country music legend Ernest Tubb (and his Texas Troubadours) sang of a "Waltz Across Texas" and delighted the world with his self-penned "Walkin' the Floor Over You" and songs such as "Slippin' Around," "Rainbow at Midnight," and "Blue Eyed Elaine." The Grand Ole Opry star opened the Ernest Tubb Record Shop in Nashville and began the Midnight Jamboree on WSM following the Opry in the late forties. Tubb's film appearances included work in Charles Starrett's The Fighting Buckeroo and Riding West. Visit www.etrecordshop.com

Moments in Time

Randall Franks and Eric Heatherly visit at Fan Fair in 2000. Among his hits were "Flowers on the Wall" and "Unforgettable."

Randall Franks and his Hollywood Hillbilly Jamboree appear in Covington, Georgia, on November 8, 2000. From left are Franks, Kim Koskela, and Barney Miller.

Randall Franks snapped this photo of the White Oak Mountain Boys in 2001 and won a Georgia Press Association photography award for capturing the unique image.

Hot Sausage Cornbread

½ lb. hot country sausage
2 cups self-rising cornmeal
1 ½ cups buttermilk
¼ cup self-rising flour
¾ cup vegetable oil
1 tsp. sugar
1 egg

Preheat oven to 450°. Combine cornmeal, flour, and sugar in bowl. Form a well in the middle. In it, drop 1 egg and pour in enough buttermilk to make pourable batter. Brown sausage in oil, then add it and half cup oil to batter. Pour batter into a hot skillet. Bake skillet in 450° oven for 25 minutes or until golden brown on top. Do not overcook. Enjoy!

Bill Lowery
Mandolinist
Guinness Book of World Record Achiever
Atlanta Country Music Hall of Honor

Moments in Time

Randall Franks and Dan Biggers led Carroll O'Connor's memorial service in Covington, Georgia, in 2001. Franks and Biggers pose next to a light post placed in his memory.

From left, Dan Biggers, Dee Shaw, and Randall Franks gather at Covington Square in 2001. The Square was the focal point of many "In the Heat of the Night" scenes.

Randall Franks and singer/actress Kassie DePaiva visit at Fan Fair 2001. DePaiva is best known for her role as "Blair Daimler Cramer" on "One Life to Live."

Covington 3-Day Coconut Cake

18 oz. box of
Duncan Hines ®
Butter Cake Mix
2 cups
powdered sugar
16 oz. container
of sour cream
12 oz. container of
frozen coconut
1 ½ cups frozen
whipped topping (Cool
Whip ®)

Grady Spradley

Grady Spradley (left) and the late Carroll O'Connor pause on the set of In the Heat of The Night in the early 1990s.
In addition to appearing in other movies, Spradley was O'Connor's photo double on the series.

Mix cake mix according to directions and bake in round pans. When completely cool, split layers in half. To make the frosting, combine the powdered sugar, sour cream, and coconut and blend well. Chill the frosting. Once chilled, reserve one cup of the frosting to use later. Spread the remainder of the frosting between the cooled cake layers and assemble the cake. Fold Cool Whip into the 1 cup of frosting. Blend until smooth. Spread on top and the sides of the cake. Seal cake in an airtight container (Tupperware container is ideal) for 3 days in the refrigerator before serving.

Grady Spradley, Photo Double for Carroll O'Connor In the Heat of the Night

Moments in Time

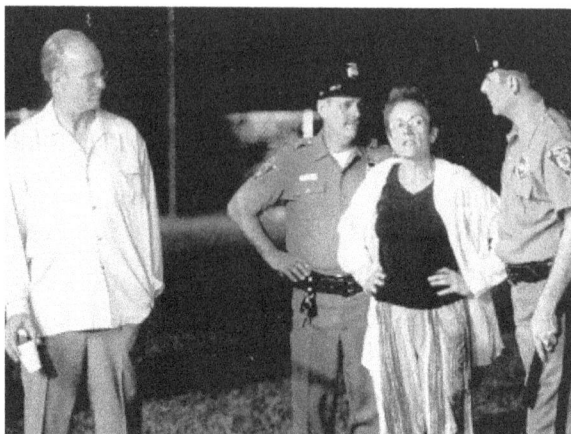

Director Martha Coolidge sets the scene for William Hurt and Randall Franks in Hallmark Hall of Fame's 50th Anniversary film "The Flamingo Rising."

© 2001 Randall Franks Media Hallmark Anthony Neste

© 2001 Randall Franks Media - Mary Miller

Randall Franks and his Hollywood Hillbilly Jamboree with Gary Waldrep (left) and Marty Hays perform for the Georgia DARE Officer's Convention in Varnell, Georgia, in 2001.

Randall Franks and actor Dennis Fimple visit at the Asheville Film Festival. Fimple starred in series such as "Alias Smith and Jones," "Matt Houston," and "Harts of the West."

© 2001 Randall Franks Media

280

Mom's Tough Egg Noodles

1 cup flour
½ teaspoon salt
1 teaspoon baking powder
1 egg
½ to 1/3 cup of milk
2 quarts chicken or beef broth

Mix together thoroughly the flour, salt, and baking powder. Add the egg and enough milk so that the mixture is stiff enough to roll out; roll the dough 1/8-inch to ¼-inch thick. Cut into ½-inch strips. Boil the noodles in the chicken or beef broth for 15 to 20 minutes. Do not prepare the mixture in advance — only just before cooking. This was a favorite dish from my youth. Serves 4.

Mac Wiseman
Bluegrass and Country Music Artist

Moments in Time

Randall Franks makes a special appearance with Gary Waldrep on the Ringgold Opry in 2001.

Randall Franks volunteers with the Catoosa Citizens for Literacy, serving on its task force and later as its chairman.

Randall Franks covers the 2002 Interstate 75 traffic accident in Ringgold, Georgia, that included nearly 90 vehicles, 40 injuries and several fatalities.

Whisper Biscuits

1 package dry yeast
¼ cup warm water
3 cups all purpose flour
1 tsp. baking powder
½ tsp. baking soda
1 tsp. salt
1 tbsp. sugar
½ cup vegetable oil
1 cup buttermilk

Dissolve yeast in warm water, let stand 5 minutes.
Combine flour and next 4 ingredients. Add yeast mixture,
oil, and buttermilk. Stir until dry ingredients are mois-
tened. Turn dough out onto a lightly floured surface. Roll
to ½-inch thickness. Cut and place on ungreased baking
sheet. Let rise in a warm place until doubled in thickness.
Bake at 400° for 15 minutes or until lightly browned.
Dough can be refrigerated for 3 or 4 days before baking.

Bill Anderson
Country Music Artist

Moments in Time

Randall Franks was honored in 2002 by Kentucky for his contributions to the music of Bill Monroe. Randall and his mother Pearl show the presentation.

Randall Franks and Pearl Franks visit with U.S. Senator Max Cleland of Georgia.

Randall Franks visits with Gospel Hall of Famer Eva Mae LeFevre (1917–2009) backstage in Chattanooga, Tennessee, in 2003.

Zucchini-Tomato Delight

2 or 3 tender, fresh zucchini squash
2 or 3 large, fresh from the garden, tomatoes
2 large sweet Vidalia onions (or purple onions)
1 large package shredded cheddar-jack cheese
Butter
Fresh basil
Salt and pepper
Bread crumbs

Grease a 9-inch by 13-inch glass casserole dish with butter or margarine. Thinly slice zucchini, tomato and onion. Layer the dish with zucchini, salt and pepper, then tomato, then onion. Sprinkle a layer of shredded cheese, and dot with thin slices of butter. Add small sprinkles of basil to each trio of veggies. Repeat until the dish is full. Finish by sprinkling cheese, bread crumbs and dots of butter over top. Cover with a tent of foil and bake at 350° for 35 minutes. Uncover and bake 10 minutes more until veggies are tender and topping is golden. Serve with warm fresh bread or biscuits for lunch or as a vegetable dish for dinner.

Gloria Gaither
Gospel Music Artist and Songwriter

Moments in Time

Randall Franks and Pearl attend the 2004 Georgy Awards in Atlanta, Georgia.

WTTI radio personalities and Randall Franks (right), Raymond Fairchild (center) and honor radio host Otis Head (second from left) at the Wink Theater in Dalton, Georgia, in 2004.

Randall Franks autographs copies of "Stirring Up Success with a Southern Flavor" at an event in Dalton, Georgia, in 2004.

Old Timey Baked Rice Pudding

3 slightly beaten eggs
2 cups milk
1½ cups cooked rice
½ cup sugar
½ cup raisins
1 tsp. vanilla
Ground cinnamon for sprinkling

Combine eggs, milk, rice, sugar, raisins, vanilla, and 1/2 tsp. salt; mix well. Bake in 10-inch by 6-inch by 2-inch dish at 325° for 25 minutes, Stir. Sprinkle with cinnamon. Continue to bake 20 to 25 minutes longer. After knife inserted halfway between center and edge comes out clean, it is done.

For topping: 2 teaspoons sugar mixed with 1 teaspoon cinnamon. Sprinkle over cooked pudding.

Place under the broiler until brown. Watch closely as top browns quick. Serve warm or chilled with light cream. Makes 6 to 8 servings.

Raymond Fairchild
Bluegrass Music Artist
Submitted by Shirley Fairchild

Moments in Time

Randall Franks is designated Catoosa County's Appalachian Ambassador of the Fiddle by the Catoosa County Commissioners in 2004.

© 2004 Randall Franks Media

© 2004 Randall Franks Media

Randall Franks is inducted into the Atlanta Country Music Hall of Fame in 2004 alongside gospel legend Charles Key (1926–2010). "Doc" Tommy Scott (left) and Johnny Carson participate.

Randall Franks brings his Hollywood Hillbilly Jamboree to the square in Covington, Georgia, in 2004 where "In the Heat of the Night" was filmed.

© 2004 Randall Franks Media – Mary Miller

Sweet Potato Souffle

3 cups cooked sweet potatoes
1 tsp. vanilla
1 cup sugar
1 egg
¼ cup milk
3 tbsp. flour
1/2 cup margarine or butter
1 tsp. cinnamon

Melt margarine or butter. Mash sweet potatoes. Mix all ingredients with potatoes and place in buttered baking dish.

Topping
1 1/3 cups brown sugar
1/3 cup plain flour
1 cup coconut (optional)
½ stick margarine or butter
1 cup chopped nuts

Melt margarine or butter. Mix ingredients in a bowl and and spread over top. Bake at 325° for 45 minutes.

Judy Watkins
The Watkins Family
Gospel Music Artist

Moments in Time

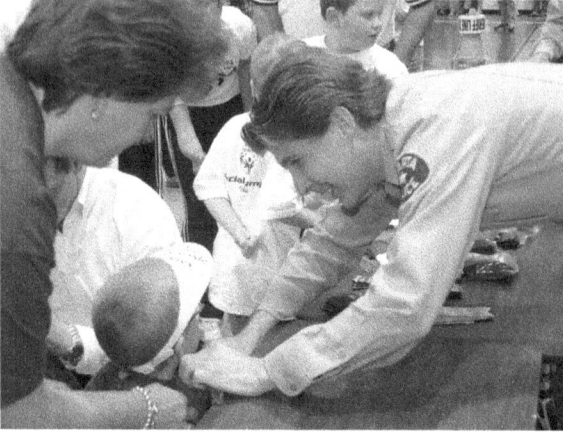

Randall Franks pins an award on a Special Olympian in Ringgold, Georgia, in 2003.

Authors Randall Franks and Shirley Smith present Catoosa County commissioners with "Stirring Up Success with a Southern Flavor" in 2003.

Randall Franks shares his Hollywood Hillbilly Jamboree for the Catoosa County 150th Anniversary Fair.

Green Pea Salad

2 8-oz. cans green peas
6 medium boiled eggs cut in slices
1 large onion, diced
4 tbsp. sweet pickle salad cubes

Mix ingredients. Salt and pepper to taste. Add mayonnaise to desired thickness.
Serve cold.

Jerry Robinson, Sr.
Vice President
Share America Foundation, Inc.
www.shareamericafoundation.org

Moments in Time

Catoosa Citizens for Literacy Executive Director Shirley Smith honors Randall Franks for service to improving the literacy of Catoosa County in 2005.

Randall Franks is honored for service to the Alhambra Shrine and the Lexington Children's Hospital in 2006. From left are Cindy and Patrick Sharrock, Franks, Joe Turner, and Brady Hughes.

The Marksmen Quartet were among the stars to honor Pearl Franks at a Concert of Celebration in June 2006 to start the Pearl and Floyd Franks Scholarship.

Blueberry Cream Cheese French Toast

1 large loaf of French bread
8 eggs plus 1 egg yolk
3 cups milk
1 tbsp. vanilla
1 cup sugar, divided
2 8-oz. packages cream cheese
1 can blueberry pie filling
1 tbsp. cinnamon

Spray 9-inch by 13-inch inch pan with Pam. Cut bread into 1-inch cubes. Place in pan. Mix 1/3 cup sugar with 1 tablespoon of cinnamon; sprinkle over bread cubes. Beat together 8 eggs, 1 tablespoon vanilla, 1/3 cup sugar and milk; pour over bread. Press bread lightly with a spatula to make sure the cubes are soaked in the egg mixture. Beat together cream cheese, 1/3 cup sugar and 1 egg yolk. Spread over bread mixture. Spread pie filling over cream cheese. Cover and refrigerate overnight. Bake uncovered at 350° for 1 hour. Let cool 10 minutes before slicing.

Jan and George Hendrix
Ringgold, Georgia

Moments in Time

Randall Franks and his mother Pearl Franks are honored by Shirley Smith on the CCL charitable fundraising success of "Stirring Up Success with a Southern Flavor."

Georgia Music Hall of Fame Curator Joseph Johnson watches Randall Franks play dulcimer at the 2005 opening of an exhibit featuring him at the Georgia Welcome Center on Interstate 75.

Randall Franks, Pearl Franks, and Georgia Senator Jeff Mullis at the Georgia Music Hall of Fame Awards in Atlanta in 2005.

McCloud's Pesto Sauce

2 ½ cups firmly packed fresh basil leaves, chopped
2 large garlic cloves
½ cup chopped walnuts, almonds, or pine nuts
½ cup fresh, grated parmesan cheese (1 ounce)
½ cup olive oil
Salt to taste (use sparingly)
Angel hair pasta

Mix basil, garlic, nuts, and parmesan in a blender or food processor until blended thoroughly.
Then add the olive oil in a slow, steady stream until a smooth paste is formed. Go easy on the oil.
Mix in with a serving of angel hair pasta. You might want to add a small amount of canola margarine to make the mixture a bit more wet. Mix to your own specifications. If you like, add additional fresh parmesan. Pesto may be refrigerated for several weeks in an airtight jar. Cover sauce with a thin layer of olive oil to prevent discoloration.

Dennis Weaver
Actor
Submitted by Gerry Weaver

Moments in Time

1890s Day Jamboree Fiddle Contest Randall Franks Trophy 2006 winner Johnny Ray Watts, Randall Franks, and runners-up Aerin DeJarnette and the senior fiddle winner.

© 2006 Randall Franks Media

© 2006 Randall Franks Media

Randall Franks receives the Little Jimmy Dempsey Award in 2006 from the Atlanta Society of Entertainers. Presenting are Phyllis Cole and Johnny Carson.

Randall Franks joins the Boynton Lions Club.

© 2007 Randall Franks Media

"Dixie Hoedown" Strawberry Shortcake

3 cups sifted all-purpose flour
4 ½ tsp. baking powder
2 tbsp. sugar (if desired)
1 ½ tsp. of salt
¾ cup shortening
1 cup milk
2 quarts fresh strawberries, hulled, cut in quarters, and sweetened
Butter
Half and half
Whipped cream

Sift the dry ingredients together and cut in the shortening. Add the milk and mix to form soft dough.
Knead lightly for 20 seconds. Divide the dough in half. Put half into a greased 9-inch layer pan. Spread a thin coating of shortening over the dough in the pan and cover with the rest of the dough, patting to fit pan.
Bake at 425° for 30 minutes. Separate the layers. Spread the bottom layer with butter and cover with half the strawberries. Place the upper layer on top of the berries and cover with the remaining strawberries. Pour a little milk (preferably half-and-half) over the shortcake and serve topped with whipped cream. Makes 10 to 12 servings.

Jesse McReynolds
Bluegrass Music Artist

Moments in Time

Pianist Paul Brown (right) and Dale Tilley perform at the Concert of Celebration in Ringgold in 2006.

Randall Franks, "Doc" Tommy Scott, and David Davis perform "Say a Little Prayer" at the Concert of Celebration in 2006.

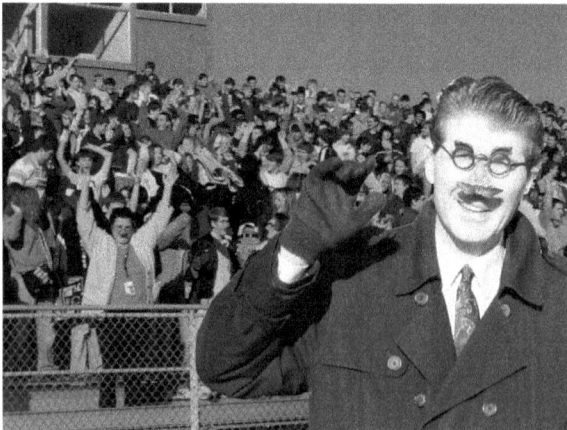

Randall Franks assists Ringgold High School students in breaking a world record related to the number of people in one location wearing Groucho glasses.

Home-Made Chili

1 lb. ground beef
¾ cup chopped onion
1 garlic clove, minced
2 tbsp. chili powder
1 tbsp. flour
1 tsp. salt
½ tsp. ground cumin
½ tsp. sugar
8-oz. can tomato sauce
1 cup water

Brown the ground beef, onion, and garlic. Drain excess fat. Stir in remaining ingredients. Mix well. Cover and simmer for 30 minutes. Makes 4 servings (About 2/3 cup each). For more servings, double the recipe.

Barbara Burn
Catoosa County, Georgia
In memory of Artist Ed Burn

Moments in Time

Randall Franks joins "Doc" Tommy Scott on stage for a Medicine Show performance at the Scopes Trial Festival at the Rhea County Courthouse in 2007.

© 2007 Randall Franks Media – Butch Lanham

© 2007 Randall Franks Media

1890s Day Jamboree Fiddle Contest Randall Franks Trophy 2007 winner Aerin DeJarnette, Randall Franks, and runners-up Ashley Sullivan and Mack Snoderly.

Producer and Manager Larry Ferguson, Dottie Rambo, and Randall Franks visit backstage in 2007.

© 2007 Randall Franks Media

Dottie's "Cat Head" Biscuits

2 ½ cups self-rising flour
2 tbsp. sugar
½ cup melted shortening
1 cup buttermilk
½ tsp. soda
½ tsp. salt

Blend flour, salt, sugar, and melted shortening. Add buttermilk to dry ingredients. Mix well with spoon and roll out on breadboard to ¾-inch thick. Cut with floured biscuit cutter. Place in greased bread pan. Brush biscuits with melted shortening. Bake at 450° for 15 to 20 minutes. Serves 12.

Dottie Rambo
Gospel Music Artist and Songwriter
Gospel Music Hall of Fame

Dottie gave me this recipe, and boy was I grateful. She really was one of the greatest cooks I've ever known. This was a fan favorite from her old Dottie Rambo Magazine Show that aired on TBN for six years.

Larry Ferguson, Dottie Rambo's former manager

Moments in Time

Randall Franks performs at the Scopes Trial Festival in Dayton, Tennessee, in 2007. From left, are Butch Lanham, Franks, Lynn Haas, and Barney Miller.

Randall Franks joins members of his family and Richard Cornelius (left) at Randall's exhibit in the Scopes Trial Museum in the Rhea County Courthouse in 2007.

"Doc" Tommy Scott (left) and Randall Franks visit with Randall's uncle Jay Hinch on the courthouse lawn in Dayton, Tennessee, in 2007.

Mama's Stovetop Pot Roast

2 ½ to 3 ½ lb. beef roast   1 large onion
Salt and pepper to taste   Potatoes
Flour   Carrots
Vegetable oil

Wash meat. While wet, salt and pepper both sides and roll in flour until covered well. Cover bottom of Dutch oven with oil and heat on medium high. Brown all sides of the meat for a few minutes. Flour will brown and some will fall off of the roast. Remove roast from the pot. Add more oil and flour and brown like you are making gravy. (Mama always said to brown it 'til you might have browned it too long … makes better gravy!) Add 8 to 10 cups of water, stir well, and put roast back in the pot. Reduce heat to medium and cover pot. Cook for about 2 hours or until the meat is done and tender. Turn meat occasionally, adding more water as needed. When meat is done, remove from pot. You should have a good amount of juice/gravy in the pot. Make a flour-water paste and whisk in slowly to avoid lumps till it reaches your desired thickness. Season to taste. If you want, add 6 to 8 small potatoes (cut in half or quartered), 4 to 6 medium carrots (peeled and cut in 3-inch pieces) and 1 large onion. Add them in the last hour of cooking. (When Mama cooked a larger roast, she would add another onion and make mashed potatoes and carrots separately.)

(Pat White's Recipe)
Cheryl White Warren
The Whites
Country Music Artist

Moments in Time

Randall Franks performs with fellow Blue Grass Boys in Bristol, Virginia, in 2007. From left are Blake Williams, Franks, Wayne Lewis, Tom Ewing, and Virginia Boy Raymond McClain.

© 2007 Randall Franks Media

© 2007 Randall Franks Media

Randall Franks and gospel singer Jerry Trammell perform in Carnesville, Georgia, in 2007. Trammell sang hits such as "Standing on the Solid Rock."

Randall Franks joins a cast of talented actors for a stage production of "Smoke on the Mountain" at the Catoosa Colonnade in 2007.

Catoosa Community Players

"Plains Special" Cheese Ring

1 lb. grated sharp cheese
1 cup finely chopped nuts
1 cup mayonnaise
1 small onion, finely grated
Strawberry preserves (optional)

Combine all ingredients, except preserves. Season to taste with pepper. Mix well and place in a 5- or 6-cup lightly greased ring mold. Refrigerate until firm for several hours or overnight. To serve, unmold, and if desired, fill center with strawberry preserves, or serve plain with crackers.

Rosalynn Carter
Former First Lady of the United States

Moments in Time

Randall Franks performs at the Fiddlin' John Carson Birthday Celebration at Sylvester Cemetery in Atlanta, Georgia, in 2007.

© 2007 Randall Franks Media

Randall Franks's perspective of half of the audience at Hominy Valley, North Carolina, where he performed as a guest of The Marksmen Quartet on July 4, 2007.

© 2007 Randall Franks Media

© 2007 Share America Foundation

Randall Franks entertains with gospel singers Buddy and Esther Liles and his wife at the Ringgold Depot in 2007. Buddy is best known for his work with the Florida Boys.

Super Low-Cal Strawberry Shortcakes

2 quarts fresh strawberries
1 large box of sugar-free Strawberry Banana Jell-O
12 ready-made shortcakes
1 pint Lite Cool Whip topping

Stem, wash, drain, then halve the strawberries. Set aside in large mixing bowl. Prepare (as directed on box) the sugar-free* Jell-O, but use only one cup of hot water. Mix the gelatin well, stirring until the gelatin is only lukewarm and beginning to thicken. Add the fresh strawberries and gently mix for approximately 3 minutes. Spoon generously over each shortcake and top with a large dollop of Lite Cool Whip topping. Serve Immediately and enjoy! This recipe will serve approximately 12 people.

*Calories per normal servings will equal less than 150. Fat content is zero for gelatin and berries, but the content for the overall recipe depends on the type of shortcake you use.
Sheb Wooley
Actor/ Country Music Artist
Submitted by Linda Dotson-Wooley

Moments in Time

Joe Turner (left) and Randall Franks (right) present fiddler Deborah Taylor as the first Pearl and Floyd Franks Scholarship Catoosa County designee in 2007.

© 2007 Share America Foundation

Randall Franks leads a chorus of musicians and attendees at the first Ringgold Depot Sacred Sounds Fridays on May 11, 2007.

© 2007 Share America Foundation

Randall Franks joins Testimony Quartet. From left Tim Owens, Heath Allen, Franks, Dove nominee Howard Stewart, and Ken Hicks of US 101 radio.

© 2007 Share America – Joe Turner

Maccheroni "all'Ultima Moda 1841" alla Napoletana

(Pasta "In the Latest Style Naples 1841")

¾ cup olive oil

1 lb. of any short tubular pasta, preferably imported Italian

3 lbs. imported Italian canned tomatoes, including the juice; or

4 lbs. very ripe summer tomatoes

Salt

Black pepper, freshly ground

½ cup parmigiano, freshly grated

Pour the olive oil into a crockery bowl. Add the pasta and mix very well. Let the pasta soak in the oil for about 20 minutes. Preheat oven to 400°. Add the canned tomatoes and all the juice to the bowl along with salt and pepper to taste. Mix very well, then transfer to a Pyrex casserole 14 inches in diameter. Bake for about 45 minutes, mixing 2 or 3 times. (If tomatoes are fresh, cut them into half-inch thick slices and alternate layers of tomato and pasta with tomatoes as top and bottom layers. Do not mix even while baking). Remove the casserole from the oven and sprinkle the cheese over the pasta mixture. Mix very well and then transfer to a serving dish. Serve immediately without adding extra cheese. Serves 4 to 6.

Alan Alda, Actor, Author, Director, Writer

Alan Alda

Television Hall of Fame member Alan Alda cut his way into the fabric of American experience through his role as surgeon "Hawkeye Pierce" in the TV series M*A*S*H. That was just a piece of the long tapestry that he has woven on and off stage, screen, and television as a performer, writer, and director. He has been nominated for an Emmy thirty-two times. In 2006, he garnered a nomination for an Emmy for West Wing, a Tony for Glengarry Glen Ross, and an Oscar for The Aviator in the same year. He has won six Emmys in his career. He is also a best-selling author with his book "Never Have Your Dog Stuffed, and Other Things I've Learned." Visit www.alanalda.com.

Moments in Time

Randall Franks with Georgia Governor Sonny Perdue and First Lady Mary Perdue in 2007.

Randall Franks performs on TV's Atlanta Live in 2007 with musicians, from left, Mark Bramlett, Barney Miller, Bill Burdette, and Bill Everett.

Randall Franks is welcomed into the Kiwanis Club of Ringgold by President Phil Erli.

Crab Chowder

¼ tsp. minced garlic
1/8 tsp. cayenne
¼ cup green pepper
1 tbsp. butter
2 cans potato soup
1 package of cream cheese
1 ½ cans evaporated milk
6 oz. crab meat
1 can whole kernel corn
Chopped onions
1/8 cup sugar

Cook onions, garlic, peppers, and cayenne in butter. Blend in soup, cream cheese, and milk. Add crab meat. Add undrained corn. Bring to a boil. Reduce heat; simmer 10 minutes. Stir in sugar.

Mary Perdue
Former First Lady of Georgia

Moments in Time

Joe Turner (left) and Randall Franks (right) present fiddler John Rice the first Pearl and Floyd Franks Scholarship in 2007.

Randall Franks performs with Dottie Rambo Scholar Garrett Arb in 2007 at the Ringgold Depot.

Joe Turner (left) and Randall Franks (right) present banjo player Jarrod Payne with the Pearl and Floyd Franks Scholarship in 2008.

James Earl Jones Chilean Sea Bass

10 maui onions
1 stick unsalted butter
12 roma tomatoes, seeded and chopped (or the canned, drained or equivalent)
5 chopped shallots
3 minced cloves garlic
3 chopped basil leaves
1 tbsp. extra virgin olive oil
½ cup chicken broth (if necessary)
12 pieces Chilean sea bass, 2 inches wide, 2 ½ inches long

James Earl Jones

For more than fifty years, Jones' tremendous acting talents on stage and screen and his marvelous voice have endeared him to fans around the world. He won two Tony Awards and was nominated for an Oscar for his performance as "Jack Jefferson" in the 1970 film The Great White Hope. He was the voice of the villain "Darth Vader" in Star Wars and the "Mufasa" in both Lion King films.

Slice and cook onions in a skillet on low heat until caramelized (between 1 and 2 hours). Puree all ingredients except last three ingredients. Heat olive oil. Add ingredients and cook on low for 30 minutes. Add chicken broth as necessary. Season bass with salt and white pepper, to taste. Cover bass with onions and bake at 425° 10 to 12 minutes. Each of 6 servings should include one piece of bass over about 1/6 of the sauce.

James Earl Jones, Actor

Moments in Time

Bluegrass Music Hall of Fame member Pete Kuykendall and his wife Kitsy, both of Bluegrass Unlimited at the IBMA Bluegrass Awards in 2008.

© 2008 Randall Franks Media

Randall Franks performs with Steel String Session at the Ringgold Depot in 2008.

© 2008 Share America – Joe Turner

© 2008 Randall Franks Media

Bluegrass performers Bill Harrell (left) and Del McCoury visit at the 2008 IBMA Awards Reception.

Sunnyside Eggs

2 large eggs
Butter

Heat an iron pan on medium heat until handle is uncomfortably warm to hold. Butter should sizzle when applied, but not burn.

Break the egg shell gently into pan. Cover immediately. Cooking proceeds rapidly — DO NOT OVERCOOK. If whites are still liquid when cover is removed for inspection, add a few drops of water and replace cover for 45 seconds. Serve on oven-warmed plate 170°. Bon appetite.

Allan Arbus
Actor

Allan Arbus

When many TV fans think of Allan Arbus (1918-2013), what quickly comes to mind is his role as psychiatrist "Maj. Sidney Freedman" in the TV series M*A*S*H, but the actor has brought characters to life on many classic TV shows and films since the 1960s, often finding himself in the role of a doctor. Some of these shows are Wonder Woman, Hardcastle and McCormick, In the Heat of the Night, Judging Amy, NYPD Blue, and Matlock.

Moments in Time

Randall Franks appears on stage with the Lewis Family at the Conasauga Bluegrass Festival near Dalton, Georgia, in 2008.

Randall Franks (center) joins Johnny Carson, Phyllis Cole, and Helen and Jerry Burke at the grave of country music pioneer Fiddlin' John Carson in 2008.

Randall Franks entertains at the Alhambra Shrine Temple in Chattanooga, Tennessee, in 2008.

Aunt Vera's
Italian Meatballs and Sauce

Meatballs

1 lb. lean hamburger
3 eggs
1/3 cup Italian bread crumbs
1/2 cup grated Parmesan cheese
2-3 tsp. dried minced onions
2 rounded tsp. fresh minced garlic
3 shakes oregano
3 shakes basil
2 tsp. parsley flakes
1 sprinkle red pepper flakes
Salt and freshly cracked black pepper

Mix well in a large mixing bowl. Shape into 15 to 16 meatballs, large enough to fill your palm. Take large frying pan and drizzle the bottom with olive oil and heat. Lightly brown meatballs on all sides. Drain in paper towel. Meatballs may be placed in a microwave for 1 to 2 minutes to ensure the meatballs are fully cooked. Do not add pan-browned bits to sauce. Set aside.

Jesse McReynolds — Continued Page 319

Moments in Time

© 2008 Share America – Joe Turner

Randall Franks joins the Southern Sound Quartet on stage in January 2008 at the Ringgold Depot.

Randall Franks brought together a unique 2008 Christmas show for Chattanooga's elite Mountain City Club including the talents of Curtis Broadway and Chasity Jones.

© 2008 Randall Franks Media

© 2008 Randall Franks Media

Randall Franks joined entertainers Paul Puckett and Lynn Baines for A Night at the Opry in Rome, Georgia, with the Rome Winds.

Marinara Sauce

1 tsp. fresh minced garlic
28-oz. can crushed tomatoes
15-oz. can crushed tomatoes
15-oz. can tomato sauce
6-oz. can tomato paste
6-oz. can of water (to rinse all cans)

In a heavy bottomed pot (If available, use a flame tower to prevent burning.), drizzle the bottom of the pot with olive oil and heat. Just before it smokes, add fresh minced garlic and brown it lightly. Immediately add all cans of tomatoes, sauce, paste, and water before garlic burns. Stir.

1 bay leaf
1-2 tsp. of parsley
2-3 shakes of oregano
2-3 shakes of basil
1-2 tsp. dried mixed onions
1-2 pinches red pepper flakes
1-2 tsp. of fresh minced garlic
Freshly cracked black pepper and salt to taste. Do not oversalt.

Stir well. Add meatballs. Bring to a medium simmer. Lower heat and simmer on low heat for 1½ to 2 hours. Keep a lid covering pot but cocked slightly to let steam escape. When done, remove the bay leaf and serve with fresh pasta. Serves 4 to 6.

Jesse McReynolds
Bluegrass Music Artist, Submitted by Joy McReynolds

Moments in Time

Share America supporters fill the Ringgold Depot in 2008.

© 2008 Share America – Joe Turner

© 2008 Share America Foundation

Joe Turner, Adam Cathey, and Randall Franks present guitarist Jeremy Barker with the Pearl and Floyd Franks Scholarship in 2008.

Earl Eleton and Naomi Sego Reader at the 2008 Southern Gospel Music Hall of Fame induction ceremonies at Dollywood.

© 2008 Randall Franks Media

Date Balls

1 cup (2 sticks) margarine
1 cup sugar
1 8-ounce package of dates chopped
1 cup chopped nuts
2 cups Rice Krispies
1 teaspoon vanilla extract
Confectioner's sugar

In a saucepan, combine the margarine, sugar, and dates and cook over medium heat, stirring constantly. Remove the pan from the heat and add the nuts, Rice Krispies, and vanilla. Let cool. Shape into 1- to 2- inch balls and place on waxed paper. Sprinkle lightly with confectioner's sugar. These keep nicely in an airtight container.

Archie Watkins
Southern Gospel Artist
Submitted by Cindy Watkins

Moments in Time

Randall Franks on stage with the Frettin' on Faith Dulcimer Club at the Ringgold Depot in 2008.

1890s Day Jamboree Fiddle Contest Randall Franks Trophy 2008 winner Mark Ralph (right), Randall Franks, John Boulware, and Mack Snoderly.

Randall Franks performs with Mountain Faith and Jim Ricketts at the Ringgold Depot in 2008.

Broccoli, Cheese, and Rice Casserole

1 small onion, chopped
1/2 cup chopped celery
10-oz. package frozen chopped broccoli, thawed
1 tbsp. butter or margarine
8-oz. jar cheese spread or Velveta cheese
10 ¾-oz. can condensed cream of mushroom soup
5-oz. can evaporated milk
3 cups cooked rice

In a large skillet over medium heat, sauté onion, celery, and broccoli in butter for 3 to 5 minutes. Stir in cheese, soup, and milk until smooth. Place rice in greased 8-inch square baking dish. Pour cheese mixture over rice; do not stir. Bake uncovered at 325° for 25 to 30 minutes or until hot and bubbly. If everyone is going to be there, we double the recipe!

The Cox Family
Bluegrass Music Artists

About the Author

Actor/entertainer Randall Franks is best known as "Officer Randy Goode" from TV's "In the Heat of the Night," a role he performed on NBC and CBS from 1988–1993. He also starred with Robert Townsend in the series "Musical Theater of Hope" which aired on GMC (Gospel Music Channel).

He has co-starred or starred in 15 films with superstars who include Dolly Parton, Christian Slater, William Hurt, Stella Parton, and legendary western star "Doc" Tommy Scott. His

Randall Franks

© 2011 Randall Franks Media – Teryl Jackson

most recent film is "Lukewarm" with John Schneider, Nicole Gale Anderson, and Bill Cobbs.

Franks' musical stylings have been heard in 150 countries and by more than 25 million Americans. The Independent Country Music Hall of Fame member's musical career boasts 20 album releases, 21 singles, and over 200 recordings with artists from various genres. The International Bluegrass Music Museum Legend annually hosts the historic Grand Master Fiddler Championship at the Country Music Hall of Fame in Nashville, Tennessee. The award-winning fiddler's best-selling release, "Handshakes and Smiles," was a top 20 Christian music seller. Many of his albums were among the top 30 bluegrass recordings of their release year. The Atlanta Country Music Hall of Fame member shared a top country vocal collaboration with Grand Ole Opry stars The Whites. In addition to his solo career, which includes 13 years guest starring for the Grand Ole Opry, Franks is a former member of Bill Monroe's Blue Grass Boys and Jim and Jesse's Virginia Boys. He has performed with Jeff & Sheri Easter, the Lewis Family, the Marksmen Quartet, the Watkins Family, Elaine and Shorty, "Doc" Tommy Scott's Last Real Old Time Medicine Show, and Doodle and the Golden River Grass.

He serves on the Ringgold City Council in Ringgold, Georgia, and

About the Author

is past chairman of the Catoosa Citizens for Literacy, which assists individuals in learning to read and pursuing a GED at its Catoosa County Learning Center near Ringgold. He is also president of the Share America Foundation, Inc. that provides the Pearl and Floyd Franks Scholarship to musicians continuing the traditional music of Appalachia. He hosts a monthly concert series at the historic Ringgold Depot which helps fund the scholarships. He is the Northwest Georgia Joint Economic Development Authority film industry liaison. He also serves as Georgia Production Partnership secretary.

He authored six other books, including "Whittlin' and Fiddlin' My Own Way : The Violet Hensley Story" with Violet Hensley; "Encouragers I: Finding the Light," "A Mountain Pearl: Appalachian Reminiscing and Recipes;" "Stirring Up Success with a Southern Flavor," and "Stirring Up Additional Success with a Southern Flavor" with Shirley Smith; and "Snake Oil, Superstars and Me" with "Doc" Tommy Scott and Shirley Swiesz.

A journalist with more than 20 state and national awards, Franks is also a syndicated columnist with his "Southern Style" appearing weekly in newspapers from North Carolina to Texas and at http://randallfranks.com/. He was included among his generation's leading country humorists in the Loyal Jones book "Country Music Humorists and Comedians."

For more information, visit www.randallfranks.com and www.shareamericafoundation.org.

Be sure to visit on the web:
Randall Franks on Twitter
https://twitter.com/RandallFranks
Randall Franks Fan Page on Facebook
www.facebook.com/pages/Randall-Franks/41082829233
Randall Franks on YouTube:
http://www.youtube.com/user/randallfranks
Randall Franks at IMDB:
http://www.imdb.com/name/nm0291684/
Randall Franks on Uplifting TV:
http://www.uptv.com/tv/actor/randall-franks

Photographers

A tremendously important aspect of my career is the visual images created to document the experiences. Since the early days with photos snapped by my mother or father or the parents of my fellow Peachtree Pickers such as Wayne W. Daniel, Neal or Emily Freeman, or Bud Earnest, my entertainment career has been documented by numerous talented friends, fans, and professionals who have included me in their passion of taking pictures. You will find many of their works included within this series with their credits where applicable. Four primary photographers followed various aspects of my career with their lenses and I wish to express my sincere thanks to them for helping to document my life in photos with such dedication and love for their craft.

Donna Tracy — Tracy is a retired nurse who served much of her career in the Alvin C. York V. A. Medical Center in Murfreesboro, Tennessee, after relocating from Maine where she started her career in nursing. Her love of country and bluegrass music brought her to attend the Country Music Association's and the Grand Ole Opry's Country Music Fan Fair. She volunteered for 18 years in the Jim and Jesse Fan Club booth and later in the Randall Franks Fan Club booth. Tracy met Randall while he was still in his teens and began chronicling his rise in country music alongside his contemporaries and those he saw as mentors.

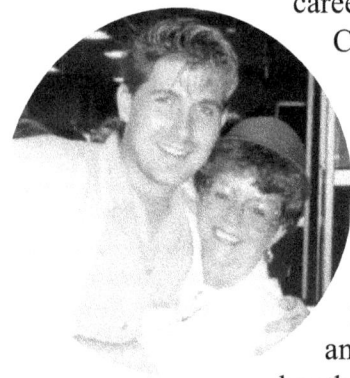

Dr. Ronald L. Stuckey — Stuckey is a retired Ohio State University professor of botany and author who had a passion for amateur photography and a love of bluegrass music. He combined his passions to amass a huge collection of images of the leading performers in the industry in the 1990s and 2000s. His works

Photographers

are now part of the collection of the International Bluegrass Music Museum.

Ned D. Burris — A professional photographer with over 32 years in the business, Burris lives in St. Mary, Ohio. Several years of his career were based in Atlanta. Some of his clientele were in the acting community. He began working with Franks early in his acting career, and their combined talents created some memorable images that appeared in fan magazines, newspapers, and other publications. Their friendship brought Burris to eventually take recording studio images and portraits of all the stars of "In the Heat of the Night" in association with Randall's production of the cast Christmas CD. His wife Donna assisted during several of the "Heat" photography sessions.

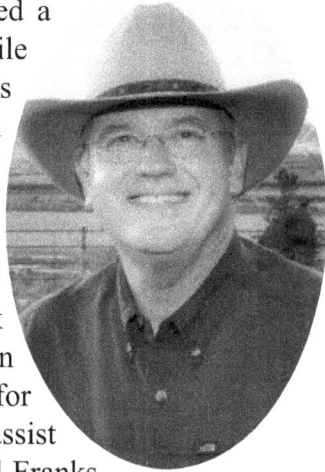

Courtesy J. Alan Palmer – 2011 Tony Esparza, CBS retired

J. Alan Palmer — Palmer developed a passion for photography as a sideline while he served as service manager in his father's Major Appliance Co. in Covington, Georgia. He took photos for the area newspapers, and his opportunities blossomed when "In the Heat of the Night" moved to his hometown of Covington, Georgia, in 1988. Palmer took numerous photos of the actors working on the set and eventually began freelancing for producers who opened doors for him to assist CBS network photographers. Palmer and Franks worked closely together, and Palmer often did special shoots for Randall on the set and around Covington.

Story Index

Story Index

Story Index

Story Index

Story Index

Story Index

Story Index

Story Index

Story Index

Story Index

Moments In Time Index

Moments in Time Index

Moments in Time Index

Recipe Index

Appetizers

Breads

Desserts

Recipe Index

Entrees

Sauces

Soups and Salads

Recipe Index

Vegetables

Celebrity Recipe Index

Don't miss the next book in this series:

Encouragers III

A Guiding Hand

www.ingramcontent.com/pod-product-compliance
Lightning Source LLC
Chambersburg PA
CBHW060243100426
42742CB00011B/1625